MW01107403

CIVIL

Laws of War Violations and
the Use of Weapons on the Israel-Lebanon Border

Human Rights Watch Arms Project

Human Rights Watch/Middle East

Human Rights Watch
New York · Washington · London · Brussels

Library of Congress Catalog Card Number: 96-76298
ISBN 1-56432-167-3

Cover photograph: Civilians in the remnants of their home, Jibshit, Lebanon, October 1993.

Human Rights Watch Arms Project
The Arms Project was established in 1992 to monitor and prevent arms transfers to governments or organizations that commit gross violations of internationally recognized human rights and the rules of war and promote freedom of information regarding arms transfers worldwide. Joost R. Hiltermann is the director; Stephen D. Goose is the program director; Ann Peters is the research associate; Kathleen A. Bleakley and Ernst Jan Hogendoorn are research assistants; William M. Arkin is a consultant; and Selamawit Demeke is the associate.

Human Rights Watch/Middle East
Human Rights Watch/Middle East was established in 1989 to monitor and promote the observance of internationally recognized human rights in the Middle East and North Africa. Christopher George is the executive director; Eric Goldstein is the research director; Joe Stork is the advocacy director; Virginia N. Sherry is associate director; Fatemeh Ziai is counsel; Elahé Hicks is a consultant; Shira Robinson and Awali Samara are associates. Gary Sick is the chair of the advisory committee and Lisa Anderson and Bruce Rabb are vice chairs.

Addresses for Human Rights Watch
485 Fifth Avenue, New York, NY 10017-6104
Tel: (212) 972-8400, Fax: (212) 972-0905, E-mail: hrwnyc@hrw.org

1522 K Street, N.W., #910, Washington, DC 20005-1202
Tel: (202) 371-6592, Fax: (202) 371-0124, E-mail: hrwdc@hrw.org

33 Islington High Street, N1 9LH London, UK
Tel: (44171) 713-1995, Fax: (44171) 713-1800, E-mail: hrwatchuk@gn.apc.org

15 Rue Van Campenhout, 1000 Brussels, Belgium
Tel: (322) 732-2009, Fax: (322) 732-0471, E-mail: hrwatcheu@gn.apc.org

Gopher Address://gopher.humanrights.org:5000
Listserv address: To subscribe to the list, send an e-mail message to majordomo@igc.apc.org with "subscribe hrw-news" in the body of the message (leave the subject line blank).

HUMAN RIGHTS WATCH

Human Rights Watch conducts human rights investigations and works to stop abuses in some seventy countries around the world. Our reputation for timely, reliable disclosures has made us an essential source of information for those concerned with human rights. We address the human rights practices of governments of all political stripes, of all geopolitical alignments, and of all ethnic and religious persuasions. Human Rights Watch defends freedom of thought and expression, due process and equal protection of the law, and a vigorous civil society; we document and denounce murders, disappearances, torture, arbitrary imprisonment, discrimination, and other abuses of internationally recognized human rights. Our goal is to hold governments accountable if they transgress the rights of their people.

Human Rights Watch began in 1978 with the founding of its Helsinki division. Today, it includes five divisions covering Africa, the Americas, Asia, the Middle East, as well as the signatories of the Helsinki accords. It also includes five collaborative projects on arms transfers, children's rights, free expression, prison conditions, and women's rights. It maintains offices in New York, Washington, Los Angeles, London, Brussels, Moscow, Dushanbe, Rio de Janeiro, and Hong Kong. Human Rights Watch is an independent, nongovernmental organization, supported by contributions from private individuals and foundations worldwide. It accepts no government funds, directly or indirectly.

The staff includes Kenneth Roth, executive director; Cynthia Brown, program director; Holly J. Burkhalter, advocacy director; Barbara Guglielmo, finance and administration director; Robert Kimzey, publications director; Jeri Laber, special advisor; Gara LaMarche, associate director; Lotte Leicht, Brussels office director; Juan Méndez, general counsel; Susan Osnos, communications director; Jemera Rone, counsel; and Joanna Weschler, United Nations representative.

The regional directors of Human Rights Watch are Peter Takirambudde, Africa; José Miguel Vivanco, Americas; Sidney Jones, Asia; Holly Cartner, Helsinki; and Christopher E. George, Middle East. The project directors are Joost R. Hiltermann, Arms Project; Lois Whitman, Children's Rights Project; Gara LaMarche, Free Expression Project; and Dorothy Q. Thomas, Women's Rights Project.

The members of the board of directors are Robert L. Bernstein, chair; Adrian W. DeWind, vice chair; Roland Algrant, Lisa Anderson, Alice L. Brown, William Carmichael, Dorothy Cullman, Gina Despres, Irene Diamond, Edith Everett, Jonathan Fanton, James C. Goodale, Jack Greenberg, Vartan Gregorian, Alice H. Henkin, Stephen L. Kass, Marina Pinto Kaufman, Bruce Klatsky, Harold Hongju Koh, Alexander MacGregor, Josh Mailman, Andrew Nathan, Jane Olson, Peter Osnos, Kathleen Peratis, Bruce Rabb, Sigrid Rausing, Orville Schell, Sid Sheinberg, Gary G. Sick, Malcolm Smith, Nahid Toubia, Maureen White, and Rosalind C. Whitehead.

CONTENTS

ACKNOWLEDGMENTS

This report is jointly prepared by the Human Rights Watch Arms Project and Human Rights Watch/Middle East. It is based on three separate research missions. Joost R. Hiltermann, the director of the Arms Project, investigated laws of war violations committed during Operation Accountability during research in Lebanon in October 1993. He was assisted by Monette Zard, a research consultant for Human Rights Watch, and Ali Srour. Stephen Goose, program director of the Arms Project, and Eric Goldstein, research director of Human Rights Watch/Middle East, jointly conducted a parallel investigation into Hizballah violations in Israel in November 1993. Virginia N. Sherry, associate director of Human Rights Watch/Middle East, investigated laws of war violations in southern Lebanon in August 1995. She was assisted by Jamal Mahroum and Ali Srour. Elizabeth Wilcox, an intern at Human Rights Watch/Middle East, did research on Operation Accountability in preparation of the two field missions in fall 1993.

Joost Hiltermann, the principal author of the report, is responsible for writing the summary and conclusions (chapter 1), the background section (chapter 2), most of chapter 5 on Operation Accountability, and the section on the use of phosphorus in chapter 6. Monette Zard wrote early versions of chapter 3 on the July 1993 "understandings" and chapter 4 on recent violations of international humanitarian law; provided input on chapter 5; and also helped with legal analysis throughout the report. Stephen Goose wrote the section on Hizballah violations in chapter 5, as well as chapter 7 on weapons transfers, with input from Kathleen Bleakley, research assistant at the Arms Project. Ernst Jan Hogendoorn, research assistant at the Arms Project, provided research, writing and editorial assistance, and wrote the section on flechettes in chapter 6. Joe Stork, advocacy director of Human Rights Watch/Middle East, provided writing and editorial input. The report was edited by Joost Hiltermann and reviewed by Virginia Sherry and other members of the Human Rights Watch/Middle East staff. Selamawit Demeke, Arms Project associate, prepared the report for publication.

Human Rights Watch is grateful to UNIFIL officers and staff for providing valuable time to our investigators. We also wish to thank the residents of southern Lebanon and Israel who welcomed us into their homes and provided testimony and other information without which this report would not have been possible.

The Arms Project acknowledges with appreciation funding from the Compton Foundation, Ruth Mott Fund, Rockefeller Foundation, and Winston Foundation for World Peace. Human Rights Watch takes sole responsibility for the contents of this report. Chapter 1 (Summary and Recommendations) of the report is available in Arabic.

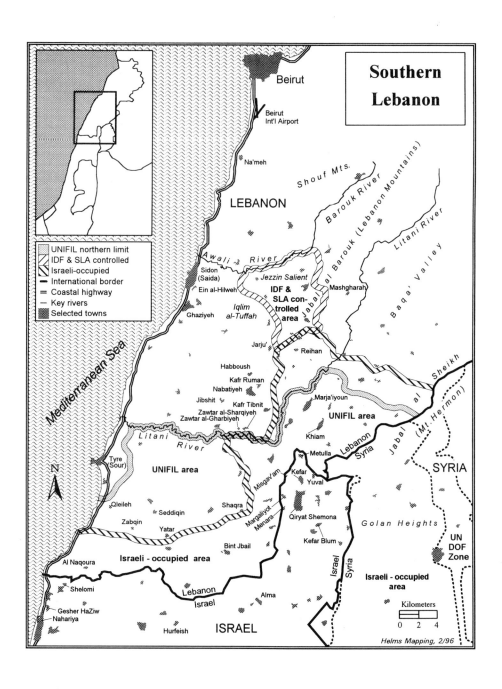

Southern Lebanon

Beirut

Beirut Int'l Airport

Na'meh

Shouf Mts.

LEBANON

Barouk River

Jabal al Barouk (Lebanon Mountains)

Litani River

UNIFIL northern limit
IDF & SLA controlled
Israeli-occupied
International border
Coastal highway
Key rivers
Selected towns

Awali River

Sidon (Saida)

Ein al-Hilweh

Jezzin Salient

Mashgharah

IDF & SLA controlled area

Iqlim al-Tuffah

Ghaziyeh

Baqa' Valley

Jarju'

Reihan

Habboush

Kafr Ruman

Nabatiyeh

Jibshit

Kafr Tibnit

Marja'iyoun

al Sheikh

Zawtar al-Sharqiyeh
Zawtar al-Gharbiyeh

UNIFIL area

Jabal (Mt. Hermon)

Mediterranean Sea

Litani River

Khiam

Metulla

Lebanon

Syria

SYRIA

N

Tyre (Sour)

UNIFIL area

Misgav'am

Kefar Yuval

Qleileh

Shaqra

Margaliyot

Menara

Qiryat Shemona

Golan Heights

UN DOF Zone

Zabqin

Seddiqin

Yatar

Kefar Blum

Bint Jbail

Israel

Syria

Al Naqoura

Israeli - occupied area

Israeli - occupied area

Lebanon

Israel

Alma

Kilometers

Shelomi

Gesher HaZiw
Nahariya

Hurfeish

ISRAEL

0   2   4

Helms Mapping, 2/96

I. SUMMARY

For over a decade, a conflict has raged on the border of Israel and Lebanon, where Israel occupies a large section of Lebanese territory. Civilians have been the principal targets and victims in this conflict. Both sides—Israel and its allied Lebanese militia, the South Lebanon Army, on one side, and guerrillas affiliated with Hizballah and a number of small Palestinian factions on the other—have exhibited a willful disregard for international humanitarian law (also known as the laws of war). Both sides have directly targeted civilians and indiscriminately lobbed shells and fired rockets at civilian population centers during various stages of the conflict.[1] Israel, with its superior firepower, has caused by far the most civilian casualties, and the most damage to residential homes and civilian infrastructure.

Although the conflict on the Israel-Lebanon border has claimed casualties on a regular basis over the years, it has received scant attention outside of the Middle East, except at times of intense escalation. During the peace negotiations between Israel and Syria that followed the 1993 Oslo accords, the matter of South Lebanon has been placed on a back burner. The apparent assumption is that once Israel and Syria, which both have a significant influence over Lebanese affairs, agree to peace, they will put a halt to the fighting on the Israel-Lebanon border as part of the overall settlement.[2]

---

[1] Because Israel has occupied foreign territory and the fighting often crosses the internationally recognized border, Human Rights Watch considers the conflict between Israel and Hizballah to be of an international character. Both sides are to be held accountable for violations of applicable international law governing the conduct of war. Both Israel and Lebanon have ratified the Geneva Conventions (1949), though not Protocol I (1977) Additional to the Geneva Conventions. Human Rights Watch considers Protocol I to be a generally accepted and authoritative elaboration of the duty to distinguish between civilians and combatants, and to spare civilians from attack. Moreover, Human Rights Watch considers Articles 51, 54 and 57 of Protocol I to be international customary law, and therefore binding upon both state and non-state actors, regardless of formal ratification.

[2] Israel's prime minister, Shimon Peres, has argued in justification for Israel's refusal to deal with the issue of South Lebanon separate from negotiations with Syria: "If there would be a real attempt on the part of the Lebanese government and the Lebanese army to guarantee that there will be just one government, just one army, and peace and security, Israel would not wait for the negotiations with the Syrians. We would withdraw before it [sic]." Voice of Israel, February 6, 1996, as recorded by the BBC Monitoring Service, February 8, 1996.

1

Short of a peace agreement between Israel and Syria, the potential for rapid escalation remains, as the Israeli assault on Lebanon in April 1996 demonstrates. Tensions are high; periods of relative calm are punctuated by sharp attacks. Since the mid-1970s, the fighting has spiraled into massive attacks back and forth on at least five occasions, gravely multiplying the humanitarian cost of the simmering conflict.[3] During the intervals, barrages back and forth have led to a situation in which no one is ever secure. As one resident of southern Lebanon put it: "Today, you are not sure whether you will be living tomorrow."[4] And referring to an intense one-week escalation in the conflict in July 1993, a resident of the Israeli town of Nahariya said: "God knows when, God knows where [the rockets] will fall next."[5]

Targeting Civilians

Civilians are not just the victims of this conflict but have been rendered pawns in the hands of the belligerents. Each side has publicly committed itself to refrain from attacking civilians, but always with a caveat—"unless the other side attacks our civilians." The threat inherent in this "unless" has been articulated on multiple occasions during the conflict and has been realized to devastating effect, turning civilians on both sides into a kind of security held in perpetual deposit. This has enabled each side to mold the enemy's behavior. Both sides have taken actions against civilians whenever the other side was seen as failing to live up to the terms of the "contract" that governed their relationship from July 1993 until April 1996.

The "contract" in question is an unwritten and informal set of rules that are based on a tacit agreement between Israel and Hizballah, brokered by the United States, that went into effect on July 31, 1993, as part of the cease-fire arrangement at the end of "Operation Accountability." They will be referred to

---

[3] The escalations referred to here are the Israeli invasion of Lebanon in 1978, known as the "Litani Operation"; the 1982 Israeli invasion of Lebanon, known as "Operation Peace for Galilee," during which Israeli troops entered Beirut and occupied vast areas of the country; the fighting between Israel and Hizballah in the wake of the killing by Israel of Hizballah leader Abbas Musawi in February 1992; the Israeli assault on southern Lebanon in July 1993, known as "Operation Accountability"; and the Israeli assault on Lebanon in April 1996, known as "Operation Grapes of Wrath."

[4] Human Rights Watch interview, Kafr Ruman, August 21, 1995.

[5] Human Rights Watch interview, Nahariya, November 21, 1993.

here as the "July 1993 understandings." The understandings supposedly prohibit attacks on civilians, but it is clear that both Israel and Hizballah have drawn a "red line." For Israel the red line is crossed if Hizballah fires Katyusha rockets across the Israel-Lebanon border, permitting the IDF—or so it is understood—to respond by shelling Lebanese villages north of the Israeli-occupied area. Hizballah has a similar red line: if the IDF or the SLA attack civilians in the south, then Hizballah would feel justified to retaliate by striking at civilian targets inside Israel. In August 1993, Israeli Prime Minister Yitzhak Rabin declared, in the words of a member of Knesset, that "Israel can only attack north of the security zone under two conditions. First, if Hizbullah violates the accord by firing Katyushas at the Galilee. In this case, Israel is not bound by any restrictions. Second, Israel can only strike north ofh the security zone...if hit first in the zone."[6] Likewise, Hizballah's deputy secretary-general, Sheikh Na'im Qasem, threatened in April 1995 that "whenever te Israeli enemy shells and harms civilians in our villages, we will shell northern Palestine and the Israeli settlements."[7] By this logic, understood by both sides to undergird their actions, both sides have accepted civilian casualties whenever their side had attacked civilians first.[8]

---

[6] David Makovsky, "Dispute on whether cease-fire limits IDF." *The Jerusalem Post*, August 2, 1993. The chairman of the Knesset's foreign affairs and defense committee, Ori Orr, added: "If it is quiet, we have no need to attack. However, if a village hits us in the security zone, the agreement says we can hit that village back." Ibid.

[7] "Hizballah Warns Israel Against Shelling Civilians," Voice of the Islamic Republic of Iran, April 29, 1995, in FBIS-NES-95-083, May 1, 1995, p. 39.

[8] Robert Fisk of *The Independent* (London) in 1995 described this agreement as follows: "Nor are the Israelis and Hizbollah in any doubt about the rules of their war in southern Lebanon. They may attack each other's military forces, but any shelling of Lebanese civilians will incur retaliatory Hizbollah rocket attacks on Galilee—an exotic reversal of the old equation whereby Israel would attack Lebanese civilians if rockets were fired into Galilee. It is now Hizbollah that adopts the eye-for-an-eye tactic....Disregarding the Hizbollah's current practice of firing Katyushas into Galilee only in response to Israeli attacks on Lebanese villages, the Israelis are now suggesting the Katyushas are fired without provocation—and that it is Hizbollah that must end its offensive in order to prevent Israeli attacks on civilians." "South Lebanon bleeds amid the talk of peace," *The Independent*, July 6, 1995. Michael Bacos Young, editor of *The Lebanon Report*, offered a similar view of the agreement. The 1993 seven-day war, he wrote, "led to an unofficial understanding—the so-called 'Damascus Agreement'—between Israel and Hizballah. The understanding 'permitted' Lebanese resistance activities in the security zone, but considered off-limits the bombardment by Hizballah of northern Israel. A subtlety was introduced in that Hizballah

This report exposes the inherent fragility of this informal understanding, which is observed mainly in the breach. Rather than serving to protect civilians, the July 1993 understandings have created a situation in which civilians are caught in a web of retaliatory violence and in which the killing of civilians has become the ultimate threat and expected response for any transgression of the agreement by either side. Air assaults, intense shelling and rocket attacks, and the indiscriminate use of lethal weapons have caused unnecessary and disproportionate civilian deaths, injuries and destruction, often either excused as "unfortunate errors" or interpreted as "permitted under the July 1993 understandings." Reprisals against civilians are specifically banned under international humanitarian law.[9]

This report is based on three separate investigations by Human Rights Watch in the region—one in southern Lebanon in October 1993; a second in northern Israel in November 1993; and a third in southern Lebanon in August 1995—as well as on research of open-source material. Human Rights Watch has found that the conflict is often brought deliberately to civilian areas, and that combatants on both sides often employ weapons in a highly indiscriminate manner. Israel, in particular, has responded to attacks on its forces in the occupied zone with shelling barrages on civilian population centers in southern Lebanon. It has done so with impunity, as the international community has remained silent whenever civilians have been targeted. An Israeli colonel, making a comparison with IDF operations in the West Bank, described the IDF's freedom of action as follows: "In south Lebanon, there is nothing between you and God Almighty. The only question you ask yourself when you are going to blow up someone's house is whether to use 50 kilos of dynamite or 25 kilos."[10] This report documents the toll taken among the civilian population, both in Lebanon and in Israel, by the frequent violation of the July 1993 understandings and the ability of both parties to act with

---

was more or less allowed to bombard northern Israel in cases in which Lebanese civilian targets were attacked." *The Lebanon Report* (Beirut), March 1995, p. 2.

[9] Article 51(6) of Protocol I declares: "Attacks against the civilian population or civilians by way of reprisals are prohibited." Likewise, Art. 33 of the fourth Geneva Convention (1949) states: "Reprisals against protected persons and their property are prohibited."

[10] Quoted by Thomas L. Friedman, "No Pain, No Gain, No Peace," *New York Times*, March 31, 1996. The colonel described the situation in the West Bank, by way of contrast, as follows: In the West Bank, "you have to explain every little move you make to 10 different people."

impunity. Since the summer of 1993, and before the massive Israeli assault of April 1996, there have been at least thirty attacks in which civilian areas were targeted by either side, often leading to loss of life and injuries.

Operation Accountability

While highlighting the impact of the fighting on civilians over the past three years, the report presents a case study of the Israeli assault on southern Lebanon in July 1993 in a military operation that is known variously as "Operation Accountability" in Israel and the "Seven-Day War" in Lebanon. Operation Accountability illustrates how the conflict on the Israel-Lebanon border can escalate and lead to great suffering among civilians. During that one short week, after a long period of relative calm, some 120 Lebanese civilians were killed and close to 500 injured by a ferocious Israeli assault on population centers in southern Lebanon, an assault which also temporarily displaced some 300,000 Lebanese villagers and Palestinian refugees.[11] In Israel, two civilians were killed and twenty-four injured in retaliatory Hizballah rocket attacks.[12] The cost of rebuilding

---

[11] These numbers were provided by the United Nations Interim Force in Lebanon (UNIFIL), "UNIFIL Updates Casualty Toll," Qol Yisra'el, July 30, 1995, in FBIS-NES-93-145, July 30, 1993, p. 45. The exact casualty toll remains unclear. Lebanese prime minister Rafiq Hariri claimed that one Lebanese soldier, eight Hizballah fighters, and 118 civilians were killed, according to David Hoffman, "Israel Halts Bombardment of Lebanon," *Washington Post*, August 1, 1993. Andrew Rathmell reported that "147 Lebanese were killed and 500 injured, the vast majority civilians," in "The War in South Lebanon," *Jane's Intelligence Review*, vol. 6, no. 4 (April 1994), p. 182. The U.S. Department of State reported that, "over 150 persons were killed and 500 wounded in Lebanon," in *Country Reports on Human Rights Practices for 1993* (February 1994), p. 1236. Israeli prime minister Yitzhak Rabin, in a briefing to the Knesset Foreign Affairs and Defense Committee, estimated that between fifty and seventy guerrillas were killed and 400 to 500 guerrillas and civilians were wounded. Reported in "Summarizes Points of 'Understanding,'" Qol Yisra'el, August 1, 1993, in FBIS-NES-93-146, August 2, 1993, p. 36. On the number of displaced, see Andrew Rathmell, "The War in South Lebanon." *Jane's Intelligence Review*, vol. 6, no. 4 (April 1994), p. 180.

[12] Col. Ahaz Ben-Ari, head of the Israel Defence Forces' international law branch, in a communication to Human Rights Watch, May 18, 1994.

destroyed and damaged homes and the infrastructure in southern Lebanon was estimated at $28.8 million.[13]
    According to statements made by Israeli civilian and military leaders, the purpose of the military operation was twofold. One was to punish Hizballah (and the militant Palestinian factions) directly. This was done through attacks on military targets, including bases, gun emplacements, and moving guerrilla groups, as well as on the homes of Hizballah leaders.[14] The second purpose was to make it difficult for Hizballah to continue using southern Lebanon as a base for attacking Israeli forces in the area occupied by Israel. This was done, as a stated goal, by deliberately inflicting serious damage on villages in southern Lebanon, through massive shelling which would raise the cost to the population of permitting Hizballah to live and operate in its midst.[15] The operation was also designed to create a refugee flow in the direction of Beirut so as to put pressure on the central government to rein in the guerrillas.[16] To the extent that civilians were the

---

[13] This was a U.N. assessment based on a interagency tour in Lebanon, August 8-13, 1993. The United Nations Department of Humanitarian Affairs, "United Nations Inter-Agency Consolidated Appeal for Emergency Humanitarian Assistance for the Population in the Conflict-Affected Areas of South Lebanon and West Bekaa," August 1993.

[14] Lt.-Gen. Ehud Barak, Israel's chief of general staff, declared: "[W]e singled out another 40 homes, mainly those of key Hizballah operatives throughout the strip of villages along the northern part of the security zone." In "Army Commanders Comment on Operation in Lebanon," IDF Radio, July 25, 1993, in FBIS-NES-93-141, July 26, 1993, p. 26.

[15] On permitting Hizballah to operate in southern Lebanon, Israel's chief of staff, Lt.-Gen. Ehud Barak, was quoted as saying: "We regard Hizballah, *the population which harbors it*, and the Lebanese regime which permits all this activity as responsible." (Emphasis added). "Rabin, Baraq Comment on Operation's Objectives." Israel Television Network, July 26, 1993, in FBIS-NES-93-142, July 27, 1993. On causing damage, Gen. Yehosh Dorfman, commander of the artillery corps, told the *New York Times* on July 28: "Now we are at the stage in which we are firing into the villages in order to cause damage to property." Chris Hedges, "Israel Keeps Pounding South Lebanon," *New York Times*, July 29, 1993. On the Israeli allegation that Hizballah has engaged in shielding, see further below.

[16] Israel's prime minister, Yitzhak Rabin, declared: "The goal of the operation is to get the southern Lebanese population to move northward, hoping that this will tell the Lebanese Government something about the refugees who may get as far north as Beirut." In "Rabin Briefs Knesset Committee on Lebanese Operation," Qol Yisra'el, July 27, 1993,

immediate targets of this military assault—to sow terror and induce behavior that would serve Israel's political goals—Israel was in grave violation of international humanitarian law. Hizballah, in retaliation, indiscriminately fired a number of Katyusha rockets across the border into northern Israel during that week, also in violation of international law.[17]

There is no doubt that civilians in southern Lebanon bore the brunt of Operation Accountability. The Lebanese authorities, local aid agencies, and international nongovernmental organizations all agreed that the vast majority of the casualties were civilians, not guerrillas affiliated with Hizballah or some of the militant Palestinian factions. The high incidence of children and older men and women on casualty lists obtained from hospitals in southern Lebanon supports this contention. The IDF has sought to justify the number of civilian casualties and the high rate of damage to civilian property by accusing Hizballah of shielding military targets with civilians. (See below). Even if guerrillas operated from within population centers, Israel is not freed from the obligation to minimize any civilian casualties resulting from its legitimate targeting of military objects. Human Rights Watch is concerned that IDF forces directed fire toward villages located closest to the source of Katyusha attacks during Operation Accountability without regard for possible civilian casualties, and possibly even as reprisal for military actions by guerrillas forces.

Moreover, although the first stage of Operation Accountability was marked by a number of precision attacks by the IDF on purported guerrilla targets, the IDF engaged in wide-scale shelling during the rest of the operation. The damage done during the shelling was then justified as necessary as a deterrent.[18] One express aim of Operation Accountability was to punish the inhabitants of

---

in FBIS-NES-93-143, July 28, 1993, pp. 20-21.

[17] Hizballah leaders have claimed that its guerrillas have fired rockets into northern Israel only in response to Israeli attacks against civilians in southern Lebanon. This claim is difficult to verify. More importantly, it is irrelevant. Under international humanitarian law, attacks on civilians cannot be justified under any circumstance, and reprisals are banned specifically.

[18] A senior IDF commander, Maj.-Gen. Me'ir Dagan, declared that "Katyushas are easy to conceal and launch, and hard to detect, thus necessitating an ongoing operation to damage the Hizballah infrastructure which would then have a deterrent effect on the organization's willingness to fire Katyushas at Israeli settlements." "IDF Deputy Operations Branch Head on Lebanon," Educational Television Network, July 26, 1993, in FBIS-NES-93-141, July 26, 1993, p. 29.

southern Lebanon for Hizballah's activities. The extensive nature of the damage sustained in numerous southern Lebanese villages confirms this stated intent.[19] Human Rights Watch has found that in addition to the large number of civilian homes damaged, the basic infrastructure of many villages had been targeted and destroyed. By the end of Operation Accountability, conservative damage estimates suggested that some 1,000 houses had been totally destroyed, 1,500 houses had been partially destroyed, and 15,000 houses had sustained light damage.[20] Israeli forces cut civilian water and electricity supplies, damaged schools, mosques and churches, and targeted a number of cemeteries with shell fire.

Human Rights Watch is concerned that although Israel issued warnings to villagers in southern Lebanon to leave their homes, these warnings were ambiguous and therefore ineffective. The content of the warnings, especially those issued during the early stages of the operation, was such as to confuse civilians about the nature of the targets selected for attack. It was therefore reasonably foreseeable that a segment of the population might not flee, and it was entirely foreseeable that in particular the old and indigent would not be able to evacuate their homes, especially considering the brevity of time between the first warnings and the beginning of the shelling. The broadcasting of warnings in no way entitled the IDF to assume that villages would be empty of a civilian population,[21] and in no way justified the conclusion of one senior Israeli officer that "as the civilian population leaves, a higher percentage of the people in the area are Hizballa [sic] terrorists as well as a few terrorists from the Palestinian organizations."[22] Unfortunately, it was actually the weakest members of the population, the elderly and the poor, who were unable to flee their villages and thereby became the principal victims of the shelling operation.

---

[19] Article 75(2)(d) of Protocol I Additional to the Geneva Conventions of 12 August 1949 prohibits collective punishment at any time and in any place whatsoever.

[20] Lebanese NGO Forum, "Humanitarian Situation: Review and Progress Report on South Lebanon," January 1994, p. 5.

[21] Maj.-Gen. Amnon Shahak, Israel's deputy chief of staff, declared on July 28, "there has been a massive flight of the population from the entire south....we estimate that most of the villages in the South have become almost totally empty." "IDF Officers Review Lebanon Operation 27 Jul" [sic], Qol Yisra'el, July 27, 1993, in FBIS-NES-93-143, July 28, 1993, p. 17.

[22] Brig.-Gen. Amir Dror of the IDF's intelligence branch, quoted in ibid.

Whether or not they chose to flee, the population of southern Lebanon became victims of the IDF's dual strategy. If they fled, they became victims of the IDF's scheme, in the words of the Israeli prime minister, Yitzhak Rabin, to "put pressure on the Beirut government and hit those who collaborate with Hezbollah."[23] But if they stayed in their homes, they fell victim to the other component of the campaign, the aim of which was, according to Gen. Yehosh Dorfman, commander of the artillery corps, "to destroy the villages and the houses of the activists and the locations from which the rockets are fired."[24]

While Israel has claimed that broadcast warnings to the civilian population in southern Lebanon were made with a view to protecting civilians from collateral injury in attacks on strictly military objectives, a number of factors make it reasonable to assume that the intention was in fact to sow terror among the civilian population. The SLA radio station broadcast threats of a general nature, warning anyone remaining in certain areas that they would be in danger of being hit. As the pattern of physical damage showed, the IDF/SLA then subjected entire villages to area bombardment. The threats and the nature of the attacks combined make clear that in significant areas in southern Lebanon whole populations—indeed anyone who failed to flee by a certain time—were targeted as if they were combatants. As the Israeli government's stated objective during Operation Accountability was to foment a refugee flow in order to put pressure on the Lebanese government to rein in Hizballah, the intention of the warnings that were broadcast and subsequent shelling is likely to have been to cause terror among the civilian population. The targeting of whole villages without distinction of specific military objectives constitutes a violation of international humanitarian law. Additionally, the issuing of warnings with the intent to cause terror also violates Article 51(2) of Protocol I, which states, in part: "Acts or threats of violence the primary purpose of which is to spread terror among the civilian population are prohibited."

In addition to subjecting villages in southern Lebanon to a massive shelling barrage during Operation Accountability, the IDF also executed what appear to have been calculated direct attacks on purely civilian targets. One such series of attacks was carried out against Sidon's wholesale vegetable market, far from the front line in south Lebanon. These attacks were executed without warning, and were probably intended both to terrify local residents into leaving

---

[23] "More Israeli Attacks Reported in South 28 Jul" [sic], AFP, July 28, 1993, in FBIS-NES-93-143, July 28, 1993, p. 36.

[24] Chris Hedges, "Israel Keeps Pounding South Lebanon," *New York Times*, July 29, 1993.

their homes and to push further northwards refugees who had sought safety in the Sidon area. At least two people were killed and six injured in the attacks on the market. The market itself was frequented by the public and the area had no apparent military or even political targets. The same intent—to instill fear—appears to have prompted the shelling attack on the adjacent Palestinian refugee camp of Ein al-Hilweh, where at least five persons were injured.

Human Rights Watch also obtained evidence suggesting that during Operation Accountability the IDF at times hindered and even attacked ambulances and vehicles of relief organizations, and carried out a number of attacks on persons attempting to flee the area. The SLA announced that the IDF would "hit all means of transportation moving on civilian and military roads" in three specified areas.[25] At least three, possibly four or five, ambulances were hit during that week. On several occasions, the Lebanese Red Cross and other recognized relief agencies were rebuffed when they requested permission from the SLA's headquarters in Marja'iyoun in the Israeli-occupied area to evacuate civilians from villages, and sometimes, when permission was granted, the time given was not sufficient to do the job. When questioned by Human Rights Watch as to the existence of a policy of blocking the population's access to relief by ordering all vehicles off the roads on pain of attack, the IDF denied ever having targeted vehicles traveling on roads in southern Lebanon.[26] Hospitals, ambulances and medical personnel are expressly protected in the Geneva Conventions of 1949.

Human Rights Watch is further concerned about the indiscriminate use by Israel of antipersonnel weapons in civilian areas. Some weapons, because of their large "kill radius," should not be used in populated areas. As this report shows, Israel has used tank-fired shells filled with flechettes in populated areas in southern Lebanon. A flechette shell is an antipersonnel weapon that contains ten to fourteen thousand 1.5-inch steel darts which, as they are released from the canister, spread out in an arc that can reach a maximum width of about ninety-four yards.[27] The

---

[25] "Israelis Warn Against Road Traffic," Voice of the South, 10:09 p.m., July 27, 1993, in FBIS-NES-93-143, July 28, 1993, p. 35.

[26] Col. Ahaz Ben-Ari, head of the IDF's international law branch, in a communication to Human Rights Watch, May 18, 1994, said: "[O]bjects of purely civilian use, such as ambulances, wounded persons being loaded into them and cemetaries [sic] were *at no stage* targeted." (Emphasis in original).

[27] Jane's Information Group, *Jane's Ammunition Handbook 1993-94* (Surrey: Jane's Information Group Limited, 1992), p. 134.

IDF has reportedly used these shells in southern Lebanon for many years, but especially in the last two years there have been repeated reports of deaths and injuries from flechettes.[28] Until recently, Israeli officials refused to acknowledge the IDF's use of these weapons, but earlier this year, after yet another Lebanese civilian was killed,[29] the Israeli minister of health, Ephraim Sneh, a former commander in southern Lebanon, admitted that flechette shells were in fact used by the IDF.[30]

Likewise, Human Rights Watch is disturbed by eyewitness testimony suggesting that Israel may have used white phosphorus, or a similar incendiary ordinarily used for marking purposes, in an antipersonnel mode in populated areas in southern Lebanon. White phosphorus ammunition, according to experts, can cause severe burns and permanent scars. During the Israeli invasion of Lebanon in 1982, the Israeli shelling of villages in southern Lebanon in July 1993, and subsequent shelling attacks, there have been numerous allegations of Israeli forces using phosphorus against civilians. The available circumstantial evidence of the illegal use of phosphorus, and/or other incendiaries, by Israel against Lebanese civilians during the 1993 events and afterwards is so compelling as to warrant serious investigation and a public response by the Israeli government. Among other evidence, Human Rights Watch saw several civilians, including children, in southern Lebanon with burns that are likely to have been caused by phosphorus.

Hizballah also violated the laws of war, indiscriminately firing Katyusha rockets into northern Israel and the Israeli-occupied area in southern Lebanon, killing and injuring a number of civilians. Hizballah's stated objective during Operation Accountability was to inflict civilian casualties and damage, thereby causing Israel to halt its air and artillery attacks—in clear violation of international law.[31] Despite the fact that overall the rockets have caused relatively limited

---

[28] Air-launched cluster bombs were used in the 1982 invasion, but Israel apparently discontinued the use of cluster bombs in southern Lebanon when the U.S. refused to supply more.

[29] "Israeli anti-personnel shell kills civilian," Reuters, December 29, 1995.

[30] "Israel confirms it uses banned shells in Lebanon," Reuters, January 1, 1996.

[31] Hassan Hoballah, head of the international relations section of Hizballah's political bureau, told Human Rights Watch: "Israel targeted civilians and we responded. We fired at Israeli settlements to press them to stop the shelling." Interview, Beirut, October 20, 1993.

damage, it is clear that attacks were intended to terrorize, and have terrorized, the civilian population in northern Israel. During Operation Accountability, tens of thousands of people fled to the south. Most people who remained were confined to community shelters or private "security rooms" for long periods of time. In some locations, women and children spent nearly twenty-four hours a day for a solid week in shelters, while men would come out only to perform essential tasks, such as feeding animals.

Although Human Rights Watch has not received any reports of civilian casualties in the Israeli-occupied zone during Operation Accountability, Hizballah appears to have fired a number of Katyushas at populated areas inside the zone. Apparently one of the main targets there was the town of Marja'iyoun. Reportedly, forty Katyushas fell in and around the town during what was described as "a week of terror." Rockets landed every day, but at different times, and people were very afraid. Schools were closed and most people stayed inside in secure rooms.

Human Rights Watch is also concerned that Hizballah may have endangered the lives of Lebanese civilians in the areas in which it has been operating. Israel's then-chief of general staff, Lt.-Gen. Ehud Barak, said on July 26, 1993: "We believe that those elements who...fire at us from within civilian settlements are responsible for the civilian casualties [and] Hizballah is responsible for the suffering caused to the civilian population which is being driven out of its homes because it continues firing at us from inside and from the outskirts of Lebanese villages."[32] Human Rights Watch is not in a position to say whether Hizballah has fired from within civilian population centers, although we are aware of cases in which Hizballah appears to have fired from within the vicinity of civilian population centers. However, as the party that is shelling and bombarding these civilian areas, the IDF is obliged not merely to assert but to provide proof that Hizballah guerrillas and other combatants in southern Lebanon have in fact used villages as shields for military activities—just as it is obliged to show that the civilian damage inflicted in southern Lebanon was proportionate to the military advantage gained.

Moreover, there have been allegations that Hizballah has carried out military activity, including military planning, in villages, and Human Rights Watch has documented at least one case in which Hizballah had stored weapons in a house in a village in southern Lebanon. In doing so, Hizballah is probably in violation of the injunction in international humanitarian law to avoid, to the maximum extent feasible, locating military objectives within or near densely populated areas and the

---

[32] "Baraq: Hizballah Responsible for Action," Qol Yisra'el, July 26, 1993, in FBIS-NES-93-141, July 26, 1993, p. 28.

parallel injunction against using civilians as a shield for military objectives or operations.

International Support for Israel and Hizballah

In addition to highlighting the violations of the laws of war that have taken place during the ongoing conflict on the Israel-Lebanon border, this report also seeks to put the spotlight on those who have aided and abetted the conflict by providing military and economic support to the belligerents—Iran and Syria in the case of Hizballah; the United States in the case of Israel. The United States is the major military patron for Israel, and Israel is by far the number one recipient of U.S. military aid. In all, Israel has received more than $40 billion in military aid from the U.S. No other country is remotely close to Israel's level of military aid. For each of the past ten years, Congress has appropriated $1.8 billion in military grants for Israel. In the most recent fiscal year, FY1996, Israel's $1.8 billion represented 56 percent of all U.S. military aid. During the course of the 1990s, U.S. military assistance has been used primarily for the procurement of and follow-on support for F-15 and F-16 fighter aircraft, F-4 fighter aircraft upgrades, Apache attack helicopters, SAAR corvettes, and the Israeli-produced Merkava tank. Funds have also been used to enhance Israeli intelligence gathering and early warning capabilities.

Owing to this generosity of the U.S., Israel also ranks as one of the biggest customers for U.S. arms sales. Over the past five years, Israel has purchased nearly $4 billion in U.S. weapons, equipment and defense services. The U.S. Government estimates that over the next two years (FY1996-97), Israel will buy $890 million in arms through the government-to-government sales channel, and $1.4 billion through the private commercial sales channel. The weaponry that Israel has used most extensively in violations of the laws of war in southern Lebanon are fighter aircraft, attack helicopters, and artillery. As the supplier of much of this weaponry, the U.S. must share the responsibility for its misuse.

The European Union, too, has a share of responsibility for Israeli actions through its trade association with Israel. In November 1995, the Commission of the European Communities and Israel concluded an association agreement. Article 2 of the agreement stipulates: "Relations between the Parties, as well as all the provisions of the Agreement itself, shall be based on respect for human rights and democratic principles, which guides their internal and international policy and constitutes an essential element of this Agreement." Under this agreement, the member states of the European Union are enjoined to remind Israel of its human rights obligations, including in its conflict in southern Lebanon.

As for Hizballah, it is frequently alleged that it has received most of its weaponry from Iran, through Syria, although few details are publicly available. Hizballah's arsenal has been reported to include armored personnel carriers, multiple rocket launchers, rocket launchers, recoilless launchers, antitank weapons (including the AT-3 Sagger guided missile), antiaircraft guns, SA-7 antiaircraft missiles, and a wide range of light weapons and small arms such as rocket-propelled grenades, machine guns, assault rifles, grenades, and landmines.[33] There are additional reports that Iran supplied Milan antitank missiles to Hizballah, and possibly also U.S. Stinger shoulder-fired antiaircraft missiles obtained from Afghanistan.[34] Iran is also reported to have supplied Hizballah with BM-21 rocket launchers—commonly known as Katyushas—throughout the 1980s.[35] According to Israel, the majority of Katyushas fired into Israel during Operation Accountability were from single round launchers "manufactured in China and North Korea as well as in Iran."[36] While the "kill radius" of a single-round Katyusha rocket is small, a volley of forty rockets is clearly able to cover a large area. As employed by Hizballah in northern Israel, the Katyushas have had an indiscriminate effect, and its use by Hizballah therefore clearly violates the injunction against indiscriminate attacks in Article 51 of Protocol I.

Recent Events

The situation in southern Lebanon since 1985 has been one of stalemate. Syria maintains some 35,000 to 40,000 troops in Lebanon, and has since extended its political hegemony over the country. While no Syrian troops have been

---

[33] Edward C. Ezell, *Small Arms World Report*, vol. 4, no. 4 (December 1993), p. 26, and International Institute for Strategic Studies, *The Military Balance 1995-96* (London: Oxford University Press, 1995), p. 140.

[34] Magnus Ranstorp, "Hezbollah's Future?" *Jane's Intelligence Review*, vol. 7, no. 1 (January 1995), p. 35. Ranstorp also reported that Syria had tried to limit shipments of arms from Iran to Hizballah in a meeting of Iran's minister of intelligence and Syria's chief of staff in Beirut in late 1994, and added: "Hezbollah circumvents these limits through the purchase of advanced weaponry, particularly AT-3s, from various arms dealers in Lebanon. Even if arms shipments from Iran ceased, it is estimated that Hezbollah has an arsenal that would enable it to continue its current level of military activity for at least five years." Ibid.

[35] Ibid.

[36] Col. Ahaz Ben-Ari, head of the IDF's international law branch, in a communication to Human Rights Watch, May 18, 1994.

deployed south of the Awali river, the Lebanese Army has gradually extended its presence throughout the south. Yet it has made no attempt to rein in Hizballah. Referring to military operations by Hizballah and other guerrilla organizations, the Lebanese prime minister, Rafiq Hariri, has stated: "The resistance...is not made by the Lebanese government. It is made by the people. All we are saying is that the people have the right to fight the occupation."[37] The Lebanese government has continued to call for a complete Israeli withdrawal from Lebanon. Hizballah, which has asserted the right to resist Israel's occupation,[38] has begun to transform itself from resistance movement to opposition party with a defined political agenda and representation in parliament. By controlling Hizballah's prime access to arms, Syria appears to hold considerable influence over Hizballah's ability to remain an active military force in the South.

There is no indication that Israel and Hizballah have been in direct negotiation over their operations in southern Lebanon. Israel, however, has negotiated with Syria, arguing that Syria has been in a position to control Hizballah's operations in southern Lebanon. The issue of peace in Lebanon has thus been subordinated to an overall peace settlement between Syria and Israel. In the spring of 1996, negotiations between Israel and Syria were suspended, and no immediate agreement was expected prior to the Israeli national elections on May 29.

In April 1996, the de facto cease-fire that had ended the July 1993 fighting broke down under the weight of cumulative violations by both sides of the agreement not to target the adversary's civilian population. Between March 4 and April 10, five weeks of attacks and reprisals had killed seven Israeli soldiers, three Lebanese civilians and at least one Hizballah fighter.[39] The tally of injured was sixteen Israeli soldiers, seven Lebanese civilians, and six Israeli civilians. The attacks came during the Israeli election campaign and brought extra pressure on the

---

[37] John Lancaster, "S. Lebanon Is Last Israeli-Arab Battleground," *Washington Post*, January 22, 1996.

[38] Hizballah's Hassan Hoballah told Human Rights Watch: "Hizballah has been fighting the Israeli occupation of southern Lebanon since 1982. We have the right to resist, by God and by law. Israel continues to occupy an area of Lebanon, about half of southern Lebanon, more than 1,000 square kilometers. We will continue to resist the occupation until liberation." Interview, Beirut, October 20, 1993.

[39] "Lebanon: Main Events in Recent Hizbollah-Israel Violence," Reuters, April 11, 1996.

Labor Party-led coalition government to respond militarily against Hizballah without regard for the limitations implicit in the July 1993 understandings. On April 9, Israel's deputy defense minister, Ori Orr, warned Lebanese civilians, referring to the July 1993 understandings: "It is clear that these rules of the game are not good and cannot remain and it is necessary that the Lebanese population living north of the security zone will live under more fear than it lives today,"[40] while Maj.-Gen. Amiram Levine declared: "[T]he residents in south Lebanon who are under the responsibility of Hizbullah will be hit harder, and the Hizbullah will be hit harder, and we will find the way to act correctly and quickly."[41] Within forty-eight hours, Israel launched what it referred to as "Operation Grapes of Wrath."

On April 11, Israel launched air and artillery attacks against what it claimed were Hizballah military and infrastructural targets, including a helicopter gunship attack on a building housing the Hizballah consultative council, or *shura*, in a southern Beirut suburb.[42] These attacks killed three Lebanese civilians and one Lebanese soldier. Following renewed Hizballah Katyusha attacks on northern Israel, Israel issued warnings, via the SLA radio station, to civilians in forty-four villages and towns in southern Lebanon, including the city of Nabatiyeh, to leave their homes by 2:30 p.m. the next day, April 12.[43] U.N. sources in southern Lebanon reported that the attacks that commenced around 4:30 p.m. were heavier and less discriminating than the attacks with laser-guided weapons on Thursday.[44] Attacks also continued against targets in Beirut and elsewhere, and one Syrian

---

[40] Shlomi Afriat, "Israel vows retaliation for Lebanon rocket attacks." Reuters, April 9, 1996.

[41] Derek Brown, "Lebanon accord in jeopardy," *The Guardian* (London), April 10, 1996.

[42] Israel claims to have hit the *shura* building. A Reuters dispatch of April 11 ("Four Dead in Israeli Attacks on Lebanon") said rather that "Israeli rockets destroyed a two-storey building next to the building of the Shura...." A Reuters dispatch the next day, April 12 ("Israel Arch Foe Hizbollah—Tough Nut to Crack") also reported that the Council building "escaped a direct hit."

[43] "Israel Steps Up Lebanese Attacks," *Washington Post*, April 13, 1996, p. A23.

[44] Ibid.

soldier was killed and seven wounded in an attack on a highway military post near Beirut's international airport.[45]

The next day, April 13, Israeli warships initiated a blockade against Beirut, Sidon and Tyre, Lebanon's chief ports of entry. The same day, an Israeli helicopter gunship rocketed an ambulance carrying fleeing civilians near Tyre, killing two women and four children and bringing the death toll to at least twenty-one people, by the estimate of Lebanese journalists.[46] Israeli government spokesman Uri Dromi declared that "We gave the residents advance warning to clear out so as not to get hurt. All those who remain there, do so at their own risk because we assume they're connected with Hizbollah."[47] On April 14, an army spokesman said: "Anyone remaining in Tyre or these forty villages [which had been named in warnings]...is solely responsible for endangering his life."[48]

By Monday, April 15, Israeli/SLA warnings to flee had been extended to a total of eighty-six Lebanese communities. As in July 1993, such warnings were in part designed to provoke a major humanitarian crisis by internally displacing upwards of 400,000 Lebanese civilians. "Even if you tie me up and whip me, I'm

---

[45] Ibid.

[46] "Israel Expands Retaliation on Lebanon," *Washington Post*, April 14, 1996, pp. A1, A26. A27. This dispatch also cites the eyewitness account of the ambulance attack by Reuters correspondent Najla Abu Jahjah. Lt.-Gen. Amnon Shahak, Israel's chief of general staff, said that "the ambulance hit in Tyre was to the best of our knowledge transporting a Hezbollah terrorist from one Hezbollah position in the area of Tyre to another." He added that "when all the details will be known, it will be conclusively proven that the target was Hezbollah terrorists using the ambulance for their own needs." According to Abu Jahjah, the vehicle was marked with the logo of the Islamic Scouts Association, an offshoot of Amal, a rival Shi'a group to Hizballah. Israel has yet to provide the evidence it claims to have for its assertion.

In an interview published in the *Washington Post* on April 17 ("Rocket Shatters a Family," p. A29), Abbas Jihah, the driver, whose wife and three daughters were among those killed, said "I believe in God and everything, but there's no way I would be involved with Hizballah." He claimed that he "was trying to help needy people and get my family out of danger. If I were Hizballah, I would not have been in the ambulance carrying bread or trying to save my family. It would have been too dangerous." An interview with Jihah also appeared in the *Los Angeles Times* on the same day.

[47] "Israel Says Checking Report on Ambulance Attack," Reuters, April 13, 1996.

[48] "Israel Extends Deadline for Tyre Evacuation," Reuters, April 14, 1996.

not going to admit on-the-record that our policy is to force out civilians to put pressure on the Lebanese government," one Israeli official told the *Wall Street Journal*. "But let's just say we hope Lebanon understands the message."[49]

Meanwhile, Hizballah reprisals, in the form of Katyusha salvos into northern Israel, continued without respite. On Sunday, April 14, Israel attacked a electric power station in Jumhour, just outside Beirut, and on Monday, April 15, struck a power station in Bsaleem in the eastern part of Beirut, asserting that the attacks were in response to an earlier Hizballah rocket attack. An Israeli army spokesman characterized the Hizballah attack, which reportedly cut an electric cable to a synagogue in Kiryat Shemona, as an attack on "electrical infrastructure in northern Israel."[50]

On April 18, an Israeli strike on a village near Nabatiyeh destroyed a building, killing a woman, her seven children and a cousin. A few hours later, Israeli artillery shells hit a makeshift refugee compound at a UNIFIL post in Qana, some ten kilometers south of Tyre, killing more than 100 displaced civilians who had fled their homes.

Prior to the carnage on April 18, the death toll and destruction had been mounting, along with evidence that Israeli forces were carrying out indiscriminate and disproportionate attacks against civilians in what had become virtual "free-fire" zones across large swaths of the south. The *Jerusalem Post* reported the "strong protest" that the U.N. had lodged with the IDF when "planes had dropped bombs in front of a clearly marked two-vehicle U.N. convoy trying to take essential items to refugees taking shelter in and around U.N. positions."[51] The onslaught in the area southeast of Tyre was particularly ferocious. On April 15, over 700 shells and 30 air-to-surface missiles and bombs poured down in a four-hour period, the U.N.

---

[49] "Lebanese Civilians Become Israel's Pawns," *Wall Street Journal,* April 16, 1996, p. A11.

[50] "If It's Lights Out for Israeli Synagogue, Beirut Must Go Dark Too," *Washington Post*, April 16, 1996, p. A11. The article, datelined Kiryat Shemona, noted that between Thursday, April 11, and Monday, April 15, some 140 Katyushas had fallen on Israel, while Israel had "fired more than 5,000 rounds of artillery into Lebanon and flown many hundereds of bombing sorties."

[51] David Rudge, "Two wounded in Katyusha attacks," *The Jerusalem Post*, April 18, 1996.

said.[52]   Journalists were unable to investigate the destruction in villages near Tyre "because of the intense bombing and shelling," Reuters reported on April 16.[53] Reuters correspondent Haitham Haddadin filed a dispatch from Tyre that day, extensively quoting residents who had fled nearby villages. "It's random shelling....They are sparing nothing. They are hitting homes and fields and civilians," one said. Up to one hundred shells, bombs and rockets were landing every hour in the village of Mansouri, a resident claimed, noting that "about 20 big guns" overlooking the village were "firing incredibly fast."[54]

These attacks, and the stated positions that accompanied them, put Israel in violation of the laws of war, which impose upon the attacker the duty to discriminate at all times between civilians and military targets. Civilians who cannot or will not flee areas that an attacker has ordered evacuated—such as the elderly, the infirm, and women with newborn children—do not automatically lose their protection under the laws of war. Nor can the attacker simply assume that those left behind are combatants and therefore subject to attack as military targets. These long-recognized principles of civilian immunity are codified in the Geneva Conventions, and subsequent restatements of customary international humanitarian law, in compellingly clear terms.

The death toll from the April 18 attack on the peacekeeping base at Qana stood at 102 civilians as of April 24. According to *The Independent*, five of the shells that landed at the base on the afternoon of April 18 were believed to be 155mm shells fired by U.S.-made M-109 self-propelled howitzers.[55] In a later report, citing the U.N., *The Independent* stated that six 155mm shells landed within the UNIFIL compound and between fifty and sixty shells landed in Qana on April 18. "According to U.N. sources in Lebanon, the Israeli shells were fitted with

---

[52] "Israel Hits Lebanon Again, US Offers Peace Plan," Reuters, April 16, 1996, citing UNIFIL sources.

[53] Ibid.

[54] Haitham Haddadin, "Israeli Blitz Spares Nothing," Reuters, April 16, 1996.

[55] Christopher Bellamy, "Lebanon: Artillery 'Cock-Up' Costs Scores of Lebanese Lives," *The Independent*, April 19, 1996.

M732 radar fuses, which detonate them at [seven meters] off the ground, the most lethal possible height, blasting fragments downwards to amputate, maim and kill."[56]

Following the attack, Lt.-Gen. Amnon Shahak, Israel's chief of staff, defended the shelling by dismissing long-established, internationally accepted laws of war. "I don't see any mistake in judgment....We fought Hizballah there [in Qana], and when they fire on us, we will fire at them to defend ourselves....I don't know any other rules of the game, either for the army or for civilians," he said at a press conference in Tel Aviv on April 18.[57]

Gen. Shahak was referring to the provocation that brought on the protracted Israeli response. A U.N. spokeswoman had confirmed that, fifteen minutes before the attack, Hizballah guerrillas had fired mortars and Katyusha rockets from a position some three hundred meters from the base.[58] Both the U.S. and Israel accused Hizballah of "shielding"—the use of civilians as a cover for military activities, which is a breach of the laws of war. "Hizballah [is] using civilians as cover. That's a despicable thing to do, an evil thing," the U.S. State Department spokesperson said.[59] Prime Minister Peres cited shielding to shift blame for the massacre to Hizballah. "They used them as a shield, they used the U.N. as a shield—the U.N. admitted it," he said on April 18.[60]

----

[56] Christopher Bellamy, "Israel: Artillery Bombardment 'Defied Orders,'" *The Independent*, April 23, 1996.

[57] "Israeli Army Chief Says UN Forewarned of Shelling," Reuters, April 18, 1996.

[58] U.N. spokeswoman Sylvana Foa at the United Nations in New York said that the commander of UNIFIL "has confirmed to us that Hizbollah forces, about fifteen minutes before the Israeli shelling, fired two Katyushas and eight mortars from a position about 300 meters from the Fijian headquarters." "United Nations: Hizbollah Fired From Near U.N. Post Hit by Israel," Reuters, April 18, 1996.

[59] Steven Erlanger, "Christopher Sees Syria Chief in Bid on Lebanon Truce," *The New York Times*, April 21, 1996, quoting State Department spokesman Nicholas Burns.

[60] Serge Schmemann, "Voicing Regret, Israeli Leader Offers a Cease-Fire," *The New York Times*, April 19, 1996. In a speech to the Israeli Knesset on April 22, Peres declared: "The terrible tragedy of Kafr Kana and the suffering of Lebanon in general are entirely the fault of the terrorist organizations, first and foremost, of Hizbullah." Information Division, Israel Foreign Ministry, "Address by Prime Minister Shimon Peres to the Knesset on the IDF Operations in Lebanon," April 22, 1996.

Any acts of shielding committed by Hizballah violate humanitarian law. They do not, however, give Israel license to fire indiscriminately into a wide area that includes a U.N. base and concentrations of civilians. The Geneva-based International Committee of the Red Cross, which issues press releases only sparingly while international armed conflicts are raging, issued a strongly worded statement on April 19, in which it "firmly condemned" the Israeli shelling at Qana, and noted the "absolute ban" on indiscriminate attacks under the laws of war. The ICRC stated that Israeli orders for the evacuation of large areas of south Lebanon did not "exempt Israel from the obligation to respect the civilians still on the spot." The ICRC also noted the Israeli orders to evacuate "in this case [were] contrary to international humanitarian law."[61]

Article 58(b) of Protocol 1 instructs parties to a conflict to "avoid locating military objectives within or near densely populated areas." The protocol does not specify the precise distance where a military target must be located in order not to be "near" a densely populated area. Nor does the protocol indicate proper locations for fixed military targets—bases, permanent artillery installations, command and control centers, etc.—compared to highly mobile military targets, such as Katyusha launchers, that can quickly be moved or abandoned after firing.[62]

---

[61] "ICRC Condemns Shelling of Civilians in Southern Lebanon," Communication to the press no. 96/14, April 19, 1996.

[62] Article 51(7) of Protocol 1 defines shielding as follows: "The presence or movements of the civilian population or individual civilians shall not be used to render certain points or areas immune from military operations, in particular in attempts to shield military objectives from attacks or to shield, favour or impede military operations. The Parties to the conflict shall not direct the movement of the civilian population or individual civilians in order to attempt to shield military objectives from attacks or to shield military operations." One authoritative commentary on Protocol 1 cites as an example of shielding "cases in which civilian refugees are herded down a road either as a shield for a moving column of combatants, or to impede the movement of the adversary's columns." Other examples would include placement of military communications or command and control equipment inside a clearly marked civilian air raid shelter (this was the justification offered by the U.S. for its attack on the al-'Ameriyeh air raid shelter in Baghdad on February 13, 1991 that claimed the lives of 204 civilians. *See* Middle East Watch, *Needless Deaths in the Gulf War: Civilian Casualties During the Air Campaign and Violations of the Laws of War* (New York: Human Rights Watch, 1991), pp. 128-147), or locating combatants inside hospitals or other buildings that are protected from attack under the laws of war (Iraq used this to justify its destruction of historic Shi'a religious shrines in Najaf and Karbala in southern Iraq during the 1991 post-Operation Desert Storm uprising. See Middle East Watch, "Endless Torment: The 1991 Uprising in Iraq and Its Aftermath" (New York:

Even if Hizballah was guilty of shielding its military operations in Qana on April 18, the laws of war did not give Israeli forces unlimited license to attack indiscriminately the general area from which the guerrillas fired mortars and Katyushas. The Israeli assault on the base and its environs must be judged against two key legal requirements. Parties to an armed conflict must refrain from indiscriminate attacks (defined as operations that are not directed at a specific military objective but that strike military targets and civilian without distinction), and from disproportionate attacks (those in which the military advantage to be gained is outweighed by excessive collateral damage to civilians). Israel violated these basic principles of the laws of war when it attacked the U.N. base and its environs.

Prime Minister Shimon Peres claimed that "We did not know that several hundred people were concentrated in that camp. It came to us as a bitter surprise."[63] The claim itself is questionable. By the IDF's own account, its forces can track the movement of individual guerrillas after the firing of Katyusha rockets.[64] Given Israel's air reconnaissance over south Lebanon during Operation Grapes of Wrath, it is difficult to imagine that the presence of over 800 civilians at a U.N. base went unnoticed.

Even if Israel did not know that civilians were housed there, its assault was nonetheless a violation of the laws of war. The base itself, with 200 Fijian peacekeepers, was not a legitimate military target. British journalist Robert Fisk, who was traveling nearby with a U.N. humanitarian convoy at the time of the attack, heard the first big guns fire into Qana just after 2 p.m. Then he heard, at 2:10 p.m., an anxious Fijian soldier report on the radio: "Our headquarters are being shelled." Two minutes later, someone from the U.N. operations headquarters in Naqqoura came on the air with these words: "We are contacting the IDF." The

---

Human Rights Watch, 1992), pp. 51-56). Hizballah certainly did not "direct" the civilians to the U.N. base. They had fled their villages southeast of Tyre because of shelling and bombing by Israeli forces. U.N. personnel had earlier evacuated many of them from their homes, and housed them at the base for humanitarian reasons. In this case the prohibition against "locating military objectives within or near densely populated areas" is the more relevant one.

[63] Serge Schmemann, "Voicing Regret, Israeli Leader Offers a Cease-Fire," *The New York Times,* April 19, 1996.

[64] Note the Israeli claims cited below with regard to the IDF attack on civilian homes in Nabatiyeh al-Fowqa earlier the same day.

Fijian came back on the line, shouting: "Do you understand? They are firing on us now. The headquarters is hit." Fisk noted the time, 2:20 pm, and wrote: "There had been six incoming rounds, then more. The guns I had heard were firing a shell every five seconds. A Lebanese U.N. liaison man came on the line from the burning...headquarters. 'People are dying here. We need help.'"[65] The protracted Israeli fire at the clearly-marked base and its environs is a classic example of an indiscriminate attack under the laws of war, which forbid treating an entire area as a military target. The breach is signficant because throughout Operation Grapes of Wrath Israel widely publicized its capacity to execute surgical strikes against Hizballah.

Hours before the attack on Qana, Israeli fighter-bombers rocketed a two-story home in the southern village of Nabatiyeh al-Fowqa, killing a mother, her new-born child, six of her other children, and a relative. According to press reports, another house, thirty meters away, was also hit, injuring four children and their parents.[66] Israeli Prime Minister Shimon Peres declared: "We don't fire at buildings for no reason. We only hit at those buildings from which Katyushas were fired....But naturally Nabatiyeh was supposed to be vacant."[67] The IDF itself did not claim that Katyushas had been fired from the Nabatiyeh houses. Neither did it provide evidence to support its claim that guerrillas ran to these houses after attacking an IDF post.[68] In either case, the civilians who remained in Nabatiyeh

---

[65] Robert Fisk, "Desperate Voices Go Unheard As Shells Rain Down," *The Independent*, April 19, 1996.

[66] Maher Chmaytelli, "Mother, Eight Children Die as Israeli Air Raid Destroys Home," Agence France Presse, April 18, 1996.

[67] Serge Schmemann, "Voicing Regret, Israeli Leader Offers a Cease-Fire," *The New York Times,* April 19, 1996. In a speech to the Israeli Knesset on April 22, Peres declared: "The terrible tragedy of Kafr Kana and the suffering of Lebanon in general are entirely the fault of the terrorist organizations, first and foremost, of Hizbullah." Information Division, Israel Foreign Ministry, "Address by Prime Minister Shimon Peres to the Knesset on the IDF Operations in Lebanon," April 22, 1996.

[68] The text of the IDF spokesman's statement, dated April 18, 1996, was as follows: "This morning (Thursday), 18 April 1996, Hizballah terrorists attacked an IDF post at Ali Taher range, in the central sector of south Lebanon. Immediately after the operation, terrorists fled to the home of a Hizballah activist on outskirts of Nabatiya, south Lebanon. IAF helicopters sent to scene were fired upon by anti-aircraft fire from the area around the house to which the terrorists fled. IAF planes fired at and hit the house. IDF again warns

al-Fowqa had not forfeited protection under the laws of war, as the IDF has the duty to exercise discretion when attacking civilian houses to avoid civilian casualties excessive of the anticipated military advantage.

As this report went to press (April 25) Israeli attacks and Hizballah reprisals were well into their fifteenth day, already exceeding the duration of the war of July 1993. The casualty toll of Operation Grapes of Wrath had reached about 150 Lebanese killed and some 300 wounded, almost all of them civilians. Casualties on the Israeli side were reported by the IDF to be twenty-six injured.[69] The BBC World Service reported on April 25 that Israeli forces had destroyed sections of roads and bridges in order to impede Lebanese from attending a mass memorial gathering for those killed in Qana.

RECOMMENDATIONS

On the basis of its findings, Human Rights Watch is making a number of recommendations which focus on the need, absent a peace agreement between Israel and Syria, for public and written commitments by both Israel and Hizballah that they will not attack civilians or civilian objects during their conflict. We also remind those paying the bills and providing the hardware of their duty to make a good-faith effort to induce the warring sides to comply with their obligations under international humanitarian law.

To the Government of Israel
- Refrain from targeting or indiscriminately attacking populated areas in southern Lebanon.
- Publicly pledge to abide by the laws of war and fundamental human rights standards in the conflict in southern Lebanon, especially with regard to the targeting of civilians.
- Specifically, make a public, written commitment not to attack civilians or civilian objects, and not to make threats to do so, including in reprisal for

---

community residents to evacuate homes to avoid harm, especially while Hizballah continues to use civilians homes to operate, hide and shoot into Galilee communities and at our forces."

[69] The Israeli figure of thirty-one injured includes five treated for shock, a category that is not used when reporting Lebanese casualties. Information Division, Israel Foreign Ministry, Jerusalem, April 21, 1996.

attacks by guerrilla groups in Lebanon. This commitment, which Hizballah is asked separately to make as well, would replace the July 1993 understandings.

- Adhere to the internationally recognized principle of proportionality by only attacking targets with significant military value while weighing the civilian cost.
- Order the IDF to conduct a review of its operational guidelines used in the conflict in southern Lebanon. This review should be public and conducted by a special commission including members of the military, the Knesset and independent legal experts.
- Order the IDF to create new guidelines including strict rules on the use of air power, artillery and other potentially indiscriminate weapons. These rules should conform to internationally recognized standards.
- Investigate allegations of the use of flechette shells, white phosphorus and other incendiaries in populated areas in Lebanon, and make a public commitment to refrain from using such weapons in civilian areas.
- Investigate all alleged IDF violations of humanitarian law and international human rights. Persons suspected of violating the laws of war should be tried and sentenced. The trials and sentencing should be public.
- Ensure that the SLA, trained and supplied by Israel, is held to the same rigid standards as the IDF. The training of SLA soldiers should include intensive indoctrination in humanitarian law. The tactics, training and recruitment methods of the SLA should meet international requirements.
- Allow delegates of the International Committee of the Red Cross free and complete access to the Israeli-occupied area in southern Lebanon.

To Hizballah
- Refrain from targeting or indiscriminately attacking populated areas in Israel and the Israeli-occupied zone in southern Lebanon.
- Publicly pledge to abide by the laws of war and fundamental human rights standards in the conflict in southern Lebanon, especially with regard to the targeting of civilians.
- Specifically, make a public, written commitment not to attack civilians or civilian objects, and not to make threats to do so, including in reprisal for attacks by Israeli military forces. This commitment, which the government of Israel is asked separately to make as well, would replace the July 1993 understandings.
- Ensure that attacks are not launched from populated areas.

- Refrain from carrying out any military activity, including military planning, that would put civilians at risk in the event of a legitimate and proportionate military attack against a Hizballah target by Israel or its allies. Specifically, ensure that all Hizballah military operations, including meetings, communications, equipment and stockpiles, are located away from populated areas.
- Ensure that members of Hizballah abide by the laws of war and fundamental human rights standards.
- Investigate all allegations of violations of humanitarian law and international human rights. Hold members of Hizballah accountable for violations of the laws of war.
- Review the tactics, training and recruitment methods of Hizballah's military wing. Ensure that Hizballah fighters undergo intensive training in humanitarian law.

To the Government of Lebanon
- Use all possible means to ensure that Hizballah implements the recommendations listed above.
- Stop the supply of Katyusha rockets to Hizballah until it publicly commits itself to refrain from targeting civilians.

To the South Lebanon Army (SLA)
- Refrain from targeting or indiscriminately attacking populated areas in southern Lebanon.
- Publicly pledge to abide by the laws of war and fundamental human rights standards in the conflict in southern Lebanon, especially with regard to the targeting of civilians.
- Specifically, make a public, written commitment not to attack civilians or civilian objects, and not to make threats to do so, including in reprisal for attacks by guerrilla groups in Lebanon.
- Ensure that members of the SLA abide by the laws of war and fundamental human rights standards.
- Investigate all allegations of violations of humanitarian law and international human rights. Hold members of the SLA accountable for violations of the laws of war.
- Review the tactics, training and recruitment methods of the SLA. Ensure that SLA members undergo intensive training in humanitarian law.
- Allow delegates of the International Committee of the Red Cross free and complete access to the area under SLA control.

To the Government of the United States

- Seek public and written assurances from the government of Israel that U.S.-supplied or U.S.-designed weapons are not used by Israeli forces indiscriminately in civilian areas in Lebanon.
- Monitor the use of all U.S. arms by Israel, and make annual reports of such use public.
- Halt the supply of, and funding or support for, F-4 and F-16 fighter aircraft, Apache attack helicopters, and any artillery to Israel until the government of Israel publicly commits itself to refrain from targeting civilians and civilian property in Lebanon.
- Publicly condemn both Israel and Hizballah for threats and attacks against civilians—immediately as they occur.
- Use all possible means, including linkages of aid and trade, to persuade Israel to implement the recommendations to the Israeli government above.
- Use all possible means, including linkage of trade, to persuade the government of Syria to halt the transshipment of Katyusha rockets through its territory until Hizballah publicly commits itself to refrain from targeting civilians.

To the European Union

- Urge the government of Israel, on the basis of Israel's human rights commitments under the E.U.-Israel Association agreement, to implement the recommendations stated above.
- Use all possible means, including linkage of trade, to persuade the government of Iran to stop providing Hizballah with Katyusha rockets until Hizballah publicly commits itself to refrain from targeting civilians.
- Use all possible means, including linkage of trade, to persuade the government of Syria to halt the transshipment of Katyusha rockets through its territory until Hizballah publicly commits itself to refrain from targeting civilians.

To the Government of Syria

- Use all possible means to ensure that Hizballah implements the recommendations above.
- Halt the transshipment of Katyusha rockets through Syrian territory until Hizballah publicly commits itself to refrain from targeting civilians.

To the Government of Iran
- Use all possible means, including linkage of aid, to ensure that Hizballah implements the recommendations above.
- Stop the transfer of Katyusha rockets to Hizballah until Hizballah publicly commits itself to refrain from targeting civilians.

II. BACKGROUND TO THE CONFLICT

The fighting on the Israel-Lebanon border dates from the 1970s. In those years, the villages of southern Lebanon were drawn into a vicious cycle of violence that was not of their own making.

Since 1948, Lebanon had played host to tens of thousands of Palestinian refugees driven from their land in the war that accompanied the creation of the state of Israel.[70] Living in sprawling encampments around the Lebanese coastal cities of Tyre (Sour), Sidon (Saida), Beirut and Tripoli (Tarablus), this population, dispossessed and destitute, spawned a generation of young fighters who were prepared to die as "martyrs" in confrontations with Israel's vastly superior military forces.

Guerrilla activity in southern Lebanon commenced in the mid-1960s, when disparate groups of Palestinian commandos began launching cross-border raids into Israel. Following the defeat of the Palestinian guerrilla organizations in Jordan in 1970-71 (known as "Black September"), the militias that managed to escape the bloodshed there moved to southern Lebanon. There they entrenched themselves among the local population, especially in the Sunni Muslim areas of the Arqoub region, joining other Palestinian groups assembled under the broad banner of the Palestine Liberation Organization (PLO) in attacking targets in Israel. During the years that followed, the Palestinian presence in southern Lebanon grew to become a virtual state within a state.

Israel retaliated against Palestinian raids with artillery bombardments, aerial strikes and even ground incursions. From the beginning, its targets included both Palestinian military and civilian sites: the guerrilla organizations' bases in the Arqoub, and the refugee camps along the Lebanese littoral from which the guerrillas drew their popular support. Gradually Israeli targets also began to include Lebanese villages, and the victims were often Lebanese civilians. In September 1972, for example, in the wake of the murder of the Israeli athletes at the Summer Olympics in Munich, Israeli forces invaded southern Lebanon, reportedly killing some 140 people, including eighty civilians.[71] The aim then, as

---

[70] According to the United Nations Relief and Works Agency for Palestinian Refugees (UNRWA), the population of registered Palestinian refugees in Lebanon stood at 344,545 in 1995. UNRWA, "Guide to UNRWA," June 1995, p. 7.

[71] Ahmad Beydoun, "The South Lebanon Border Zone: A Local Perspective," *Journal of Palestine Studies*, vol. 11, no. 3 (Spring 1992), p. 39.

today, was to serve notice to the local population that a price would have to be paid for permitting the Palestinian commandos to continue to live in their midst.

The combination of the Palestinian organizations' increasingly indifferent, even arrogant, attitude toward Lebanese sensibilities and a mounting civilian casualty rate from Israeli retaliatory attacks led to a great deal of local resentment toward the Palestinians and produced political divisions in southern Lebanon that Israel exploited to great effect. In 1975, a civil war broke out in Lebanon that was to last for over fifteen years. Central power disintegrated to make way for sectarian-based militias that carved out areas of control throughout Lebanon.[72] The PLO, for its part, dominated the Arqoub region in southern Lebanon. Building on the minority Christian population's fear of the Palestinians' growing power in the south, Israel helped establish a local militia under the command of a Christian Lebanese Army officer, Major Sa'ad Haddad, in 1976. The Haddad militia promptly set about clearing the border zone of both Palestinian guerrillas and its majority Shi'a population. In the process the villages suffered terrible destruction, and some were even razed.[73] Ironically, in later years, the militia's rank-and-file would consist for a large part of young recruits from the remaining Shi'a villages who either joined for lack of employment or were pressed into service by the militia's Christian Maronite officers.[74]

An even more forceful Israeli response to Palestinian cross-border attacks was the so-called Litani Operation in March 1978, when the Israel Defense Forces (IDF) pushed as far north as the Litani river. Again, as houses were blown up and thousands of villagers became displaced, it was the civilian population that suffered most from a military campaign whose purported targets were the Palestinian

---

[72] For a more detailed account of the Lebanese civil war, see the chapter on Lebanon in Human Rights Watch, *Playing the "Communal Card": Communal Violence and Human Rights* (New York, 1995), pp. 126-41.

[73] For example, the Shi'a villages of Hanin, Marun al-Ras and al-Qantara, as well as the Sunni villages of Yarin and Marwahin were razed to the ground. Beydoun, "The South Lebanon Border Zone: A Local Perspective," p. 43. Beydoun himself was a native of the large village of Bint Jbeil, whose population was reduced from 24,000 to some 400 in late 1976. The villagers were not allowed to return until 1981.

[74] James Bruce estimates that the SLA's troops are 60 percent Shi'a, 25 percent Druze, and 15 percent Christian, in "South Lebanon's vicious little war continues to smoulder," *Janes's Intelligence Review Pointer*, vol. 2, no. 10 (October 1995), p. 3. Morale in the SLA is apparently extremely low and in a number of instances the IDF has had to station soldiers in SLA outposts to enforce discipline and prevent desertions.

guerrilla organizations.[75] President Jimmy Carter later wrote that at the time he had prepared to notify Congress, "as required by law, that U.S. weapons were being used illegally in Lebanon, which would have automatically cut off all military aid to Israel."[76] No Congressional action was ever taken, but the U.S. did play a key role in the drafting of two 1978 U.N. Security Council resolutions: Resolution 425, which called on Israel to "withdraw forthwith its forces from all Lebanese territory," and Resolution 426, which established UNIFIL, the United Nations Interim Force in Lebanon, assigned with the task of overseeing the Israeli withdrawal. Although the IDF did withdraw most of its regular forces from southern Lebanon, it handed control of the border zone (a strip about ten kilometers wide) over to the Haddad militia, which became known as the South Lebanon Army. Israel continued to support the SLA with military advisors and matériel. By the account of Avraham Tamir, former IDF general and former director-general of the foreign ministry, "huge sums of money were invested in fortifying and equipping the SLA."[77] In April 1979, Haddad announced the formation of the Free and Independent Lebanese State in the enclave which the SLA had carved out with Israel's help. Israel never relinquished its control over this zone, and enlarged it in the 1980s.

The next round in the ferocious battle between Israel and the PLO (of which southern Lebanon was not the target as much as the stage) began in 1982. In June, after a year of calm on the border, the IDF launched a wide-scale invasion, called "Operation Peace for Galilee," which sought to smash the PLO's military and political apparatus in Lebanon once and for all.[78] Thousands of civilians were

---

[75] The operation followed the hijacking of a bus by Fatah commandos in Israel. Thirty-seven civilians are reported to have died in the attack, as well as nine commandos. The casualty toll of the Litani Operation was reportedly about 1,100 dead, the great majority of them civilians. Augustus Richard Norton with Jillian Schwedler, "(In)Security Zones in South Lebanon." *Journal of Palestine Studies*, vol. 13, no. 1 (Autumn 1993), p. 65.

[76] Jimmy Carter, *The Blood of Abraham: Insights into the Middle East* (Boston: Houghton Mifflin Co., 1985), p. 97.

[77] *Yedi'ot Ahronot*, June 21, 1995, as reported in *Mideast Mirror*, June 21, 1995.

[78] One year earlier, in July 1981, Israeli air strikes in southern Lebanon prompted the PLO to retaliate, firing rockets into northern Israel, the so-called "War of the Katyushas." Thousands of Israelis were forced to flee. In response, the Israeli Air Force bombed the Fakhani district in Beirut, where the PLO's headquarters were located, reportedly killing some 300 and injuring 700, the majority of them civilians. This led to a

killed in aerial bombardments as the Israeli forces laid siege to Beirut. United Nations Security Council resolutions calling for a total, immediate and unconditional withdrawal of Israeli troops from Lebanon were brushed aside in the interest of Israel's overriding political and military objectives, and Israel continued to occupy large parts of the country.[79]

The Israeli military presence in Lebanon soon bred a home-grown Shi'a resistance based primarily in the southern suburbs of Beirut, the Beqa' valley, and the villages of southern Lebanon. The main resistance organizations were the Amal movement and Hizballah (the Party of God), each with a military wing. In 1995, Israeli prime minister Yitzhak Rabin summarized how the dynamics on the ground in the south had changed over the years of the Israeli occupation: "When the zone was established, the main problem was that of Palestinian terror groups. The main danger was the infiltration of terrorist squads into Israeli territory. Today, this problem is virtually nonexistent. This task the 'security zone' has fulfilled successfully. There are virtually no infiltrations of terrorist squads into Israeli territory or settlements, unlike the situation six or seven years ago. The problem today is not with Palestinians but Hizbollah, an extremist Islamic element."[80]

By 1985, as the IDF's losses had grown to a politically unacceptable level, the Israeli government decided to withdraw its troops from most of Lebanon, while holding on through the SLA (now headed by Major General Antoine Lahd) to a self-declared "security zone."[81] This zone was an expanded version of the enclave that Israel and the SLA had controlled jointly from 1978 to 1982, and included the sizeable Jezzin salient, a mountainous area that juts north from the Litani river into the Shouf mountain range, dividing the coastal plain to the west from the Beqa'

---

de facto Israeli-PLO cease-fire brokered by U.S. assistant secretary of state Philip Habib. Andrew Gowers and Tony Walker, *Behind the Myth: Yasser Arafat and the Palestinian Revolution* (New York: Olive Branch Press, 1991), p. 186.

[79] For the text of the relevant Security Council resolutions, see Fida Nasrallah, *The Question of South Lebanon*, Prospects for Lebanon, vol. 5 (Oxford: Centre for Lebanese Studies, 1992).

[80] Comments made to reporters while visiting wounded IDF soldiers at a hospital in Haifa, as reported in *Mideast Mirror*, October 19, 1995.

[81] Israeli casualties reportedly reached a level of one soldier killed a day in 1983-84. Beydoun, "The South Lebanon Border Zone: A Local Perspective," p. 48.

valley in the east. Since 1985, the Israeli-occupied area has covered an area of approximately 850 square kilometers (332 square miles), or 10 percent of Lebanese territory. The border dividing the zone from the rest of Lebanon runs due east from the Mediterranean coast just above al-Naqoura along the ridge between the Tyre and Bint Jbeil districts before turning north to the Litani river, paralleling the Israeli border. A few miles west of the Israeli town of Metulla, it stretches further north, extending deep into Lebanese territory, separating the Jezzin salient from the coastal plain at Sidon to the west. It then curves east across the Shouf mountain range. Once it reaches the western flank of the Beqa' valley, it turns south again before bending east to meet the border with Syria on the slopes of Jabl al-Sheikh (Mount Hermon). The SLA's positions in the Jezzin salient enabled its gunners to reach the Mediterranean shores at Sidon and control the only two-lane highway leading to Beirut from the South. Control of the highway proved highly useful to Israeli strategists in the July 1993 fighting, when the IDF/SLA succeeded in causing an enormous bottleneck just north of Sidon (see below), thereby aggravating the fear and planned havoc that they created through its massive shelling in the preceding days.

The Israeli-occupied area, which is home to a population of 150,000 living in 162 villages and towns, serves as a virtual Maginot Line for the Israeli forces. The SLA deploys between 2,500 and 3,000 soldiers there, while the IDF maintains a regular presence of about 1,000 to 1,200 soldiers.[82] Entry into the zone from the north through one of the SLA-manned checkpoints is restricted to those who have obtained a permit from the SLA. Fortified IDF/SLA observation posts, platoon-sized positions equipped with machine guns, mortars and ground surveillance radar, dot the hilltops along the dividing line. Some of these hilltop posts are as close as a mile from the nearest Lebanese village, well within the range of small arms fire.

The situation in southern Lebanon since 1985 has been one of stalemate. Israel continues to occupy part of Lebanon, facing Lebanese (and some small

---

[82] Andrew Rathmell cites the figure of "about" 2,500 SLA troops and "about" 1,000 IDF soldiers. Andrew Rathmell, "The War in South Lebanon." *Jane's Intelligence Review,* vol. 6, no. 4 (April 1994), p. 179. Associated Press routinely gives the figure of 2,500 SLA and 1,200 IDF troops in its reports, while Reuters routinely estimates the SLA's and IDF's military strength in southern Lebanon at, respectively, 3,000 and 1,000 troops. When tensions rise, the IDF rushes in more forces. There have been some press reports of the SLA suffering from many desertions, and of the IDF having to deploy more of its soldiers on the perimeter of the occupied area. For example, see Derek Brown, "Lebanon: Israeli-Backed Militia Loses Will to Fight," *The Guardian* (London), March 23, 1996.

Palestinian) resistance groups that are supported variously by Syria and Iran. The resistance groups frequently carry out attacks on IDF/SLA patrols and positions in the occupied area.[83] In retaliation, the IDF rains bombs and shells on areas where the guerrillas are suspected to be hiding. Often, Israeli targets include the villages themselves, or their immediate surroundings, leading to loss of civilian life and a paralysis in agricultural activity in the areas contiguous to the occupied zone.[84] Captured guerrillas are routinely taken to a prison camp in the village of Khiam in the Israeli-occupied area, where they are tortured at the hands of the SLA, sometimes assisted by officers of Israel's domestic intelligence service (the General Security Service, or Shin Bet).[85] Ostensibly in response to Israeli attacks on civilian areas in Lebanon, Hizballah and other guerrilla groups, for their part, have fired Katyusha rockets indiscriminately into northern Israel, causing damage and injuries, sending civilians into air-raid shelters, and paralyzing economic life.

UNIFIL's mandate is renewed routinely every six months, but the U.N. force, currently consisting of close to 5,000 soldiers, never has had an opportunity to fulfill its stated objective of overseeing the U.N.-ordered withdrawal of Israeli

---

[83] At a Knesset Foreign Affairs and Defense Committee meeting on April 25, 1995, Lt.-Gen. Amnon Shahak, Israel's chief of staff, said there were an average of fifty to sixty attacks a month in southern Lebanon. "Back to Suicide Car Bombing in South Lebanon 'Security Zone,'" *Mideast Mirror*, vol. 9, no. 79, (April 26, 1995). According to *Jane's Intelligence Review Pointer*, since Israel withdrew from most of Lebanon in 1985, more than 400 SLA militia have been killed and 1,200 wounded. Israeli casualties have been 136 killed and 400 wounded. James Bruce, "South Lebanon's vicious little war continues to smolder," *Jane's Intelligence Review Pointer*, vol. 2, no. 10 (October 1995), p. 3.

[84] An Irish UNIFIL commander interviewed in the summer of 1993 for the television program "Beirut to Bosnia," reported that houses in the village of Bra'shit had been shelled in recent days by an Israeli Merkava tank based on the nearby IDF/SLA observation post. "Beirut to Bosnia," produced and directed by Michael Dutfield of Barraclough Carey, London, for Channel Four TV, UK, and aired in three segments on December 7, 14 and 21, 1993.

[85] Amnesty International, *Israel/South Lebanon: The Khiam Detainees: Torture and Ill-Treatment* (London: 1992).

troops.[86] UNIFIL has probably had a mitigating effect on the scale and frequency of armed conflict, but has otherwise remained ineffectual in separating the adversaries. Without the mandate or the firepower to do more, UNIFIL has found itself in the unenviable position of watching the rockets and shells fly back and forth overhead, while on occasion falling victim to direct hits itself.[87]

The September 1989 Taif Accord brokered by the Arab League brought a cease-fire and gave international state sanction to a Syrian military presence in Lebanon. Following the defeat of Gen. Michel Aoun in October 1990, the Lebanese Army began to disarm the militias in the spring of 1991—with the notable exception of Hizballah whose presence in the south was seen as balancing the power of the SLA.[88] Syria maintains some 35,000 to 40,000 troops in Lebanon, and with the May 1991 Syrian-Lebanese Treaty of Brotherhood, Cooperation and Coordination extended its influence over Lebanon. While no Syrian troops have been deployed south of the Awali river, the Lebanese Army has gradually projected its presence throughout the south. Yet it has made no attempt to rein in Hizballah. Referring to military operations by Hizballah and other guerrilla organizations, the Lebanese prime minister, Rafiq Hariri, has stated: "The resistance...is not made by the Lebanese government. It is made by the people. All we are saying is that the people have the right to fight the occupation."[89] The Lebanese government has continued to call for a complete Israeli withdrawal from Lebanon.[90] Hizballah,

---

[86] In January 1996, UNIFIL had 4,649 soldiers from nine countries, as well as 561 civilian staff. United Nations Security Council, *Report of the Secretary General on the United Nations Interim Force in Lebanon*, S/1996/45 (January 22, 1996), par. 14.

[87] On December 27, 1993, for example, an Israeli Merkava tank fired on a U.N. position and killed a Norwegian UNIFIL soldier. Human Rights Watch telephone interview, UNIFIL, December 5, 1995.

[88] This is not to say that other militias have no access to arms. There are still some weapons in Palestinian refugee camps, and the Amal Movement, a rival to Hizballah, also still has weapons and has carried out attacks against the IDF and SLA.

[89] John Lancaster, "S. Lebanon Is Last Israeli-Arab Battleground," *Washington Post*, January 22, 1996.

[90] Lebanon's permanent representative to the United Nations, Samir Moubarak, has written: "In view of Israel's continued aggressions against Lebanon and their threat to the peace process, it must be underscored that the implementation of Security Council resolution 425 (1978) remains the only way to stop the violence in southern Lebanon."

which has asserted the right to resist Israel's occupation,[91] has begun to transform itself from resistance movement to opposition party with a defined political agenda and representation in parliament. It reportedly is supplied militarily by Iran via transshipment through Syria. By controlling Hizballah's prime access to arms, Syria appears to hold considerable influence over Hizballah's ability to remain an active military force in the South.[92]

There is no indication that Israel and Hizballah have been in direct negotiation over their operations in southern Lebanon. Israel, however, has negotiated with Syria, arguing that Syria has been in a position to control Hizballah's operations in southern Lebanon. The issue of peace in Lebanon has thus been subordinated to an overall peace settlement between Syria and Israel. The Syrian foreign minister, Farouq Chara', is on record as stating that "we are for calming things down" in southern Lebanon.[93] Israel's prime minister, Shimon Peres, has taken the position that "[i]f there would be a real attempt on the part of the Lebanese government and the Lebanese army to guarantee that there will be just one government, just one army, and peace and security, Israel would not wait for the negotiations with the Syrians. We would withdraw before it [sic]. The problem is that in Lebanon you have armed groups which don't take orders from the central government, like Hizballah; that the central government and the army were unable to provide security, neither to the southern part of Lebanon and, for that reason, for the northern part of Israel. We are not here willingly, and we don't have any ambition to remain here."[94] In the spring of 1996, negotiations between

---

United Nations Security Council, "Letter Dated 17 January 1996 from the Permanent Representative of Lebanon to the United Nations Addressed to the Secretary-General," S/1996/34, January 17, 1996.

[91] Hassan Hoballah, the head of the international relations section of Hizballah's political bureau, told Human Rights Watch: "Hizballah has been fighting the Israeli occupation of southern Lebanon since 1982. We have the right to resist, by God and by law. Israel continues to occupy an area of Lebanon, about half of southern Lebanon, more than 1,000 square kilometers. We will continue to resist the occupation until liberation." Interview, Beirut, October 20, 1993.

[92] See for example, Rathmell, "The War in South Lebanon," p. 181.

[93] Lancaster, "S. Lebanon Is Last Israeli-Arab Battleground."

[94] Voice of Israel, February 6, 1996, as recorded by the BBC Monitoring Service, February 8, 1996.

Israel and Syria were suspended; no immediate agreement was expected prior to the Israeli national elections on May 29.

Meanwhile, the situation in southern Lebanon turned extremely tense again after two sets of attacks back and forth in late March and early April. The attacks came during the Israeli election campaign and brought extra pressure on the Labor Party-led coalition government to act "tough" against Hizballah and ignore understandings reached with Hizballah about the rules of the conflict three years earlier. On April 9, Israel's deputy defense minister, Ori Orr, warned Lebanese civilians: "It is clear that these rules of the game are not good and cannot remain and it is necessary that the Lebanese population living north of the security zone will live under more fear than it lives today,"[95] while Maj.-Gen. Amiram Levine declared: "[T]he residents in south Lebanon who are under the responsibility of Hizbullah will be hit harder, and the Hizbullah will be hit harder, and we will find the way to act correctly and quickly."[96] On April 11, Israel launched "Operation Grapes of Wrath" in what appeared to be a replay of Operation Accountability in 1993.

---

[95] Shlomi Afriat, "Israel vows retaliation for Lebanon rocket attacks." Reuters, April 9, 1996.

[96] Derek Brown, "Lebanon accord in jeopardy," *The Guardian* (London), April 10, 1996.

III. THE JULY 1993 UNDERSTANDINGS

Since July 1993, an informal, unwritten set of rules has governed the conduct of the conflict between Israel and the SLA on one side and Hezbollah on the other. These rules are based on a tacit agreement between Israel and Hizballah that reportedly went into effect on July 31, 1993, as part of the cease-fire arrangement at the end of "Operation Accountability," and they will be referred to here as the "July 1993 understandings."[97] The agreement was brokered by U.S. Secretary of State Warren Christopher, and involved—directly or indirectly— the governments of Israel, Lebanon, Syria and Iran.[98] The understandings supposedly prohibit attacks on civilians. Israeli housing minister Binyamin Ben-Eliezer, following a cabinet meeting in Jerusalem on August 22, 1993, described the agreement this way: "We have to continue to hit Hizbullah, every place and everywhere. But we have to do it in a way not to involve civilians."[99] Hizballah had acknowledged as much in a statement it issued in Beirut when the cease-fire came into effect at the end of July: "[T]he group said it will halt its rocket attacks as long as Israeli forces do not fire on Lebanese civilians," Reuters reported.[100]

The agreement was put to the test on August 19, 1993, when Hizballah claimed responsibility for the killing of eight Israeli soldiers in two separate

---

[97] This informal understanding has also been referred to as the "July Agreement," the "Damascus Agreement," or just "the Agreement."

[98] The *Washington Post*, citing Israeli officials, reported the following about Secretary Christopher's role: "The cease-fire was brokered by Secretary of State Warren Christopher in phone calls to the leaders of Israel, Syria and Lebanon and through indirect contacts with Iran, Hezbolloh's chief sponsor." David Hoffman, "Israel Halts Bombardment of Lebanon," *Washington Post*, August 1, 1993. The spokesman for then Israeli prime minister Yitzhak Rabin, in a statement issued on July 31, acknowledged that "understandings" had been reached with Lebanon, Syria and "other powers that have influence in Lebanon." Ibid. According to Israeli officials, a senior Iranian government official who was in Damascus at the time was directly involved in the negotiations: "Israeli officials said the diplomatic contacts that led to the cease-fire had involved Iranian Foreign Minister Ali Akbar Velayati, who is in the Syrian capital, Damascus. 'I think Christopher had to make only one call—to Damascus,' an Israeli official said." Ibid.

[99] Gerald Butt, "Paying the price of failure," *Middle East International*, August 28, 1993, p. 5.

[100] Hoffman, "Israel Halts Bombardment of Lebanon."

bombings that day in the security zone. Israel retaliated with "airstrikes...aimed at Hezbollah military targets in three unpopulated sites in the Bekaa Valley."[101] Hizballah did not, in response, fire rockets into northern Israel, presumably because the Israeli reaction was limited to military targets.[102]

The various parties to the agreement have been reluctant to spell out their precise involvement in the bringing about of the "understandings" and their roles in enforcing the agreement's terms. Syrian president Hafez al-Asad has publicly acknowledged the existence of the agreement, but has stated that Syria is not a party to it.[103]   As for Israel, Lt.-Gen. Amnon Shakak, the chief of staff, has been reported as saying that Israel has no signed agreement with Hizballah but that "understandings at the time [July 1993] were reached with the United States, which talked with Syria, which talked with Hizballah, which again talked with the Syrians, who again talked with the Americans, who reported back to us."[104]   It

---

[101] Nora Boustany, "Guerrillas in Lebanon Kill 8 Israeli Soldiers," *Washington Post*, August 20, 1993.

[102] "The Israeli army chief of staff, Ehud Barak, said in a television interview tonight that the attacks fell within the informal rules set out in the cease-fire agreement, [correspondent David] Hoffman reported [from Jerusalem]. Barak said that the accord includes no restrictions on combat inside the 'security zone,' and that Hezbollah has not exceeded the terms by firing rockets into Israel. Other officials said Israel's retaliation also did not break the pact because the airstrikes were aimed at Hezbollah military targets in three unpopulated sites in the Bekaa Valley." Boustany, *Washington Post*, August 20, 1993.

[103] At a joint press conference with Egyptian president Hosni Mubarak in Damascus on April 2, 1996, Asad said this: "We know that an understanding was reached between the two sides in 1993 and Syria was not a party to it. The said understanding provides that the resistance in South Lebanon would not rocket northern Israel while Israel would not bombard civilians or civilian targets. The truth of the matter is that they in Israel do not abide by the said understanding. Anyone of you who would monitor events on the ground over a period of one week, or two weeks, or one month or two months or several years, will discover that the shelling [by Israel doesn't cease]." *Mideast Mirror*, April 3, 1996.

[104] Shahak, addressing the Knesset Foreign Affairs and Defense Committee on April 2, 1996, was quoted by "Knesset and army sources" who spoke with Qol Yisra'el. "Israel: Chief of Staff Discusses Lebanon, Hamas Attacks, Closure." FBIS-NES-96-065, April 3, 1996, p. 35. Israeli housing minister Ben-Eliezer stated on July 31 that his country's understanding with Hizballah was indirect, and based on commitments from Lebanon and Syria. According to the *Washington Post*, "While the agreement was not put

seems clear that the U.S. continues to serve as a broker between Israel and Hizballah, via the government of Hafez al-Asad in Damascus. Israeli military analyst Ze'ev Schiff, who writes for the daily newspaper *Ha'aretz*, noted recently that Israeli "apologies" for violations of the July 1993 understandings have been "delivered to Hizballah via Damascus through the Americans."[105]

Whatever the precise nature of U.S. and Syrian government involvement in orchestrating the agreement and its implementation, it is clear that both Israel and Hizballah have drawn a "red line." For Israel the red line is crossed if Hizballah fires Katyusha rockets across the Israel-Lebanon border, permitting the IDF—or so it is understood—to respond by shelling Lebanese villages north of the Israeli-occupied area. Hizballah has a similar red line: if the IDF or the SLA attack civilians in the south, then Hizballah would feel justified to retaliate by striking at civilian targets inside Israel.[106] In August 1993, Israeli Prime Minister Yitzhak

---

in writing, Israeli officials said the United States' role will help in enforcing its terms. 'I think that when I say 'understanding' between the United States and all the governments, [this] means somehow there is a commitment between the governments to the United States,' Housing Minister Binyamin Ben-Eliezer, a confidant of Rabin, told state-run radio. While Israel has no direct promises from Hezbollah, he said, the commitments of Lebanon and Syria are 'enough for me,' he added." Hoffman, "Israel Halts Bombardment of Lebanon."

[105] *Ha'aretz*, April 2, 1996, as reported in *Mideast Mirror*, April 2, 1996.

[106] Robert Fisk of *The Independent* (London) in 1995 described this agreement as follows: "Nor are the Israelis and Hizbollah in any doubt about the rules of their war in southern Lebanon. They may attack each other's military forces, but any shelling of Lebanese civilians will incur retaliatory Hizbollah rocket attacks on Galilee—an exotic reversal of the old equation whereby Israel would attack Lebanese civilians if rockets were fired into Galilee. It is now Hizbollah that adopts the eye-for-an-eye tactic....Disregarding the Hizbollah's current practice of firing Katyushas into Galilee only in response to Israeli attacks on Lebanese villages, the Israelis are now suggesting the Katyushas are fired without provocation—and that it is Hizbollah that must end its offensive in order to prevent Israeli attacks on civilians." "South Lebanon bleeds amid the talk of peace," *The Independent*, July 6, 1995. Michael Bacos Young, editor of *The Lebanon Report*, offered a similar view of the agreement. The 1993 seven-day war, he wrote, "led to an unofficial understanding—the so-called 'Damascus Agreement'—between Israel and Hizballah. The understanding 'permitted' Lebanese resistance activities in the security zone, but considered off-limits the bombardment by Hizballah of northern Israel. A subtlety was introduced in that Hizballah was more or less allowed to bombard northern Israel in cases in which Lebanese civilian targets were attacked." *The Lebanon Report* (Beirut), March 1995, p. 2.

Rabin declared, in the words of a member of Knesset, that "Israel can only attack north of the security zone under two conditions. First, if Hizbullah violates the accord by firing Katyushas at the Galilee. In this case, Israel is not bound by any restrictions. Second, Israel can only strike north of the security zone...if hit first in the zone."[107]   Likewise, Hizballah's deputy secretary-general, Sheikh Na'im Qasem, threatened in April 1995 that "whenever the Israeli enemy shells and harms civilians in our villages, we will shell northern Palestine and the Israeli settlements."[108]   A month later he was interviewed as saying: "We repeatedly said then [during the July 1993 seven-day war] that we do not fire Katyusha rockets at Israeli settlements except in retaliation for the bombardment of villagers in our regions."[109]   Haj Husein al-Khalil, head of Hizballah's political bureau, likewise declared: "We spelled out our view of the so-called July understandings...namely that if the Israeli enemy hits civilian targets, he should expect us to retaliate against civilian targets. If the Zionist enemy widens the scope of his attacks to shell villages and towns, we will respond in the appropriate way....[A]ny attack on civilians or villages or homes will meet a comparable response."[110]

---

[107] David Makovsky, "Dispute on whether cease-fire limits IDF." *The Jerusalem Post*, August 2, 1993. The chairman of the Knesset's foreign affairs and defense committee, Ori Orr, added: "If it is quiet, we have no need to attack. However, if a village hits us in the security zone, the agreement says we can hit that village back."

[108] "Hizballah Warns Israel Against Shelling Civilians," Voice of the Islamic Republic of Iran, April 29, 1995, in FBIS-NES-95-083, May 1, 1995, p. 39.

[109] *Al-Wasat*, May 29, 1995, as reported in *Mideast Mirror*, May 26, 1995 (*Al-Wasat* is a weekly appearing on Mondays. Contents are frequently quoted by *Mideast Mirror* prior to the stated date of publication).

[110] *Mideast Mirror*, December 21, 1994. At 1 a.m. on May 5, 1995, after Hizballah launched Katyushas at Kiryat Shemona in retaliation for an Israeli shelling on May 4 that had killed and wounded civilians in the village of Jarju', Qasem again repeated the group's interpretation of the July 1993 understandings: "After the 1993 devastation, we announced that the Islamic Resistance will respond to any Israeli aggression against civilians by bombarding northern Palestine. We have repeatedly said that any aggression against civilians and against our peaceful villagers will be returned by Katyusha attacks against northern Palestine. We cannot let anyone in northern Palestine live in peace so long as our own people are outside the circle of safety." "Hizballah's Qasim Defends Galilee Attack." MBC Television (London), May 5, 1995, FBIS-NES-95-088, May 8, 1995, p. 36.

By this logic, understood by both sides to undergird their actions, it should therefore perhaps not be surprising that after Israel admitted that its aircraft had mistakenly bombed a home in the village of Deir al-Zahrani in August 1994, killing seven civilians (including three children) and injuring seventeen, it decided not to respond to two days of retaliatory rocket attacks on northern Israel by Hizballah. This was in some way regarded as "an acceptable case of an eye for an eye."[111] More recently, on July 9, 1995, Hizballah fired Katyusha rockets into the western Galilee in retaliation for shelling by Israeli forces that killed three children in Nabatiyeh al-Fowqa on July 8.[112] There were no Israeli casualties from the rocket attacks and, rather than ordering a military response in southern Lebanon, Israel's chief of staff, Lt.-Gen. Amnon Shahak, issued a public apology of sorts on Israeli TV: "Yesterday we fired at the wrong place in Nabatiyeh, but that happens in the kind of war we are fighting there."[113] Three months later, Prime Minister Yitzhak Rabin noted that Israeli forces had exercised restraint and upheld their side of the July 1993 understandings following the civilian deaths in Nabatiyeh: "Since July 9, not a single Katyusha rocket was fired against the Galilee," he said after a special cabinet meeting on the killing of nine IDF soldiers in south Lebanon between October 12 and October 15. "Our main aim was to allow the Israelis and the children on summer holiday to enjoy themselves. Because of the IDF activity, it was a peaceful summer and all the understandings were kept," Rabin added.[114]

The July 1993 understandings have proven to be inherently unstable. While theoretically designed to protect civilians from attack, in reality they have offered the civilian population on either side of the border no succor. Violations of the agreement, intentional or not, have prompted back-and-forth retaliations against civilian targets, sometimes lasting for days, turning civilians in Israel and Lebanon into virtual pawns of the warmakers.[115] On June 23, 1995, for example,

---

[111] "An Agreement to Disagree," *The Lebanon Report*, May 1995, p. 6.

[112] See the section on flechettes in Chapter VI for more details about this attack.

[113] "Rebels in Lebanon Fire Rockets To Retaliate for Israeli Shelling," *Washington Post* (Reuters story), July 10, 1995.

[114] *Mideast Mirror*, October 17, 1995.

[115] In a flare-up in late March 1995 in which both sides attacked populated areas, Israeli housing minister Binyamin Ben Eliezer stated on Israeli television: "There has been an obvious infringement of the agreement, which necessitates a response." That response

at least ten Katyusha rockets hit an Israeli Club Med resort in the northern town of Nahariya, killing a French cook and wounding nine other civilians. This attack was Hizballah's retaliation for the death of a young woman caused by an Israeli bombardment of the Lebanese village of Shaqra the previous day, itself precipitated by an earlier Hizballah attack from Shaqra's outskirts against a military SLA outpost in the Israel-occupied area.[116] Israel responded to the June 23 Katyusha attack with further heavy artillery and air attacks on villages in southeastern Lebanon. The rationale for the latest wave of attacks was, according to Maj.-Gen. Amiram Levine, chief of Israel's Northern Command, that Hizballah was using Lebanese villages as cover: "If the Hezbollah thinks they will bring about a disaster for our citizens, I am convinced that in the end it will bring about a disaster on those very citizens whose welfare they seek."[117]

Interpretations of precisely what the rules are under the July 1993 understandings also may vary. On June 2, 1994, an Israeli attack on a Hizballah training camp in 'Ein Kawkab in the eastern Beqa' valley resulted in the deaths of some thirty-five persons, all alleged by Israel to be Hizballah fighters. Most of those killed were 12-to-18-year-olds attending what Israel referred to as an indoctrination camp. This attack, described by Israel's deputy defense minister, Mordechai Gur, as a "pure and successful military strike," apparently came within the ambit of the informal agreement: no civilians were targeted, and therefore no retaliation against civilians would be justified. Hizballah, however, saw the attack as directed against a civilian target and retaliated against areas in northern Israel that same day, prompting Gur to threaten that Israel would respond "seven-fold" against Hizballah villages if these attacks continued.[118]

A similar conflict over interpretation occurred in March 1995, when Rida' Yassin, one of Hizballah's military commanders in the south, was killed in an

---

was the IDF/SLA shelling of Lebanese villages. Reported by Barton Gellman, "Israel, Hezbollah Hit Civilian Areas," *Washington Post*, April 1, 1995.

[116] Barton Gellman, "Club Med on Israeli Coast Hit by Rockets Fired in Lebanon," *Washington Post*, June 24, 1995.

[117] Quoted by Gellman, ibid. If Hizballah indeed fired from within the vicinity of the village of Shaqra, it may have been in violation of international humanitarian law which prohibits military forces from launching attacks from civilian areas. See below.

[118] Samir Ghattas, "Israel bombs training base for Muslim fundamentalists," *Washington Times*, June 3, 1994.

Israeli helicopter attack. Hizballah's secretary-general, Sheikh Hassan Nasrallah, declared that the July 1993 understandings were no longer binding.[119] Hizballah then launched some thirty Katyushas into the northern Galilee. One Israeli civilian was killed and nine were wounded.[120] Because the killing of Rida' Yassin should have been "acceptable"—by Israel's interpretation—in the broad context of the agreement, Israel complained that Hizballah's attack constituted a flagrant violation of the July 1993 understandings. A subsequent Israeli retaliation wounded seven Lebanese civilians.[121] Tensions then abated. In an interview with the daily *L'Orient le Jour*, Sheikh Na'im Qasem qualified Hizballah's position by noting that the July 1993 understandings were still in effect, but that from then on the organization would consider the assassination of resistance officials within civilian surroundings a violation of the unwritten agreement.[122]

This adjustment in Hizballah's position then may explain the movement's response to the killing of another of its commanders on November 28, 1995, ostensibly by the IDF or Israeli agents. Hizballah fired some twenty Katyusha rockets toward Kiryat Shemona and areas north of Nahariya. A few Israeli civilians suffered light injuries, mainly from shock. In retaliation, according to a U.N. report, the IDF then "fired more than 600 artillery, tank and mortar rounds, causing minor material damage."[123] Interestingly, Hizballah had fired an earlier salvo of Katyushas at northern Israel prior to the killing of one of its commanders on November 28. In an apparent fudge, it later justified this attack as a response to a variety of Israeli actions in southern Lebanon. According to the U.N. report: "Hizbullah issued a communique listing a number of grievances, including the prolonged shelling, air attacks, the blockade of Lebanese fishermen and the

---

[119] Barton Gellman, "Israel, Hezbollah Hit Civilian Areas," *Washington Post,* April 1, 1995.

[120] "Guerrillas on Alert as Israel Vows Revenge,"AFP, April, 1, 1995, in FBIS-NES-95-063, April 3, 1995, p. 44. The series of attacks took place on March 31, 1995.

[121] Ibid.

[122] As paraphrased in *The Lebanon Report.* "An Agreement to Disagree," *The Lebanon Report*, May 1995, p. 6.

[123] United Nations Security Council, *Report of the Secretary General on the United Nations Interim Force in Lebanon*, par. 6(a).

demolition of houses in [the village of] Bayt Yahun, as the cause for its initial rocket salvo...."[124]

International law holds that forces must distinguish between civilians and combatants, and between civilian objects and military objectives. U.N. General Assembly Resolution 2444 (1968) expressly recognizes the customary law principle of civil immunity and its complementary principle requiring warring parties to distinguish civilians from combatants at all times, in affirming

> ...the following principles for observance by all government and other authorities responsible for action in armed conflicts:
>
> (a) that the right of the parties to a conflict to adopt means of injuring the enemy is not unlimited;
>
> (b) that it is prohibited to launch attacks against the civilian population as such;
>
> (c) that distinction must be made at all times between persons taking part in the hostilities and members of the civilian population to the effect that the latter be spared as much as possible. [125]

This principle is reiterated in Article 48 of Protocol I Additional to the Geneva Conventions of 12 August 1949.[126] Article 50(3) of the Protocol moreover specifies that the "presence within the civilian population of individuals who do not

---

[124] Ibid.

[125] Respect for Human Rights in Armed Conflicts, General Assembly Resolution 2444, 23 U.N. GAOR Supp. (No 18), p. 164, U.N. Doc. A/7433 (1968).

[126] Article 48 (Basic rule) reads: "In order to ensure respect for and protection of the civilian population and civilian objects, the Parties to the conflict shall at all times distinguish between the civilian population and combatants and between civilian objects and military objectives and accordingly shall direct their operations only against military objectives." While Israel has not ratified Protocol I, Human Rights Watch considers Protocol I as a generally accepted and authoritative elaboration of the duty to distinguish between civilians and combatants, and to spare civilians from attack. In addition, Human Rights Watch considers Articles 51, 54 and 57 to represent customary international law and therefore to be binding on Israel.

come within the definition of civilians does not deprive the population of its civilian character." In addition, the targeting of civilians as a reprisal for the enemy's attack on one's own civilian population—something implicitly envisioned by the July 1993 understandings—is clearly illegal under the laws of war. Article 51(6) of Protocol I declares: "Attacks against the civilian population or civilians by way of reprisals are prohibited."[127] Despite these prohibitions, the IDF/SLA and Hizballah have deliberately targeted civilian areas and both sides have claimed the right to retaliate in kind.

To the extent that Hizballah may have fired weapons from within the vicinity of populated areas, or has otherwise used villages as a shelter for its guerrilla forces, it may have been in violation of the prohibition on shielding. Article 58(b) of Protocol I provides that parties to the conflict must "to the maximum extent feasible...avoid locating military objectives within or near densely populated areas." Article 51(7) provides:

> The presence or movements of the civilian population or individual civilians shall not be used to render certain points or areas immune from military operations, in particular in attempts to shield military objectives from attacks or to shield, favour or impede military operations. The Parties to the conflict shall not direct the movement of the civilian population or individual civilians in order to attempt to shield military objectives from attacks or to shield military operations.

---

[127] Reprisals have been prohibited since the Geneva Conventions of 1949. Article 33 of the fourth Geneva Convention states: "Reprisals against protected persons and their property are prohibited." Reprisals are forbidden by international law because they involve retaliation with measures that are always prohibited, and often take the form of collective punishment of civilians for the acts of others. The ICRC commentary on Art. 33 states: "The prohibition of reprisals...is absolute and mandatory in character and thus cannot be interpreted as containing tacit reservations with regard to military necessity." Jean S. Pictet, ed., *Commentary: IV Geneva Convention Relative to the Protection of Civilian Persons in Time of War* (Geneva: International Committee of the Red Cross, 1958), p. 228. The ICRC commentaries on the 1949 Geneva Conventions and the 1977 Optional Protocols constitute the authoritative commentary on the background and interpretation of humanitarian law, drawing upon the record of the diplomatic conferences that drafted and agreed the four conventions and two protocols.

At the same time, even if Hizballah is found to have used civilians as shields, Israel is still bound by additional international law obligations. Article 51(8) of the Protocol provides:

> Any violation of these prohibitions shall not release the Parties to the conflict from their legal obligations with respect to the civilian population and civilians, including the obligation to take the precautionary measures provided for in Article 57.

Article 57 stipulates that combatants must take proper care to ensure the safety of civilians.

IV. RECENT VIOLATIONS OF HUMANITARIAN LAW

In 1995, appearances were deceptive in places such as Kafr Tibnit, Zawtar al-Gharbiyeh, Zawtar al-Sharqiyeh, Kafr Ruman, Humin, or Shaqra, all villages in southern Lebanon close to the front line. Life appeared normal. Children played outside. Lush gardens bloomed with hibiscus, gardenia and jasmine. Fruit ripened on pomegranate and fig trees. Villagers were busy stringing deep-green tobacco leaves, which then dried in the sun until they turned a crisp golden brown. Women walked the narrow streets, and shops were open for business. Everywhere there was activity, and the semblance of normality.

But no civilian is safe in these villages. Shelling by Israel's nearby military forces or the SLA can cut you down with shrapnel anywhere, at any time. This is simply a grim fact of life in the south. An elderly farmer who was working in his fields in Kafr Tibnit was killed by a direct hit several hours after dawn in July 1995. A twenty-three-year-old university student was killed instantly in Kafr Ruman when shelling started before dawn in February 1995. In the same attack, a thirty-seven-year-old father of six was killed in a nearby house when a shell exploded on the verandah; three of his children were injured. In May 1995, a twelve-year-old girl who was at a friend's house at the wrong time was killed, while her friend was injured.

It is the unpredictability of these attacks that is the most jarring aspect of life in the south. But residents have become so accustomed to the violence that they use the Arabic word *'adi*—ordinary, or normal—to describe military tactics that, measured against internationally accepted laws of war, constitute serious violations.

From January 1995 to mid-March 1996, sixty-four IDF and SLA soldiers were killed and 200 wounded in south Lebanon.[128] Israeli military officials claim that between 1994 and 1995 there was a sharp increase in the number of attacks on IDF/SLA military targets in south Lebanon. Israel's chief of staff, Lt.-Gen. Amnon Shahak, told the Knesset Foreign Affairs and Defense Committee on April 25, 1995, that there were some fifty to sixty attacks monthly in the south: "[T]he numbers are twice what they were this time last year. Not a day passes without an attack."[129] Hizballah attacks are routinely followed by IDF/SLA retaliation in the form of shelling or bombing of areas in which the guerrillas are said to be operating. This has included Lebanese villages. In the period since Operation

---

[128] *Ha'aretz*, March 19, 1996, as reported in *Mideast Mirror*, March 19, 1996.

[129] *Mideast Mirror*, April 26, 1995.

Accountability in July 1993, both sides to the conflict in southern Lebanon not only have carried out attacks on each other's forces but also against areas of civilian population. The following is a sampling of incidents based on a field investigation conducted by Human Rights Watch in southern Lebanon in August 1995.

Indiscriminate shelling and rocket attacks continue to take their toll of civilian casualties. Both sides frequently resort to long-range attacks, and the sound of artillery, mortar and rocket attacks is common throughout much of the region adjoining the Israel-Lebanon border. Israel's chief of staff, Lt.-Gen. Amnon Shahak, told Israeli military correspondents on October 15, 1995 that Israeli forces do not target civilian areas in south Lebanon: "We have no problems whatsoever in operating against Hizballah. The [understanding reached in July 1993] does not prevent us taking the initiative against Hizballah. We do not target civilian villages."[130] Despite this assertion, IDF/SLA shells, fired deliberately or otherwise, have landed in populated areas and caused civilian casualties. UNIFIL has estimated that 37,000 artillery, mortar and tank rounds were fired by the IDF/SLA in 1995.[131] In 1995 some seventeen Lebanese civilians lost their lives and dozens more were wounded as a result of IDF/SLA shelling.[132] Similarly, Hizballah fired Katyusha rockets into northern Israel on several occasions in 1995, causing two civilian deaths and thirty-one injuries.[133]

"We're used to it," said Ghassan Tabaja, as he showed Human Rights Watch an unexploded shell that had landed in his backyard in the village of Kafr Tibnit at 8:30 a.m. on August 21, 1995. The shell was embedded in the red soil less than twenty meters from the verandah where his children were playing. He pointed to a nearby house that was hit by another shell in the same barrage. He said that over one hundred shells had landed in and around the village during a

---

[130] *Mideast Mirror*, October 15, 1995.

[131] Human Rights Watch telephone interview with UNIFIL spokesperson, January 31, 1996.

[132] Lebanese civilian dies of injuries in south Lebanon," Reuters, January 18, 1996.

[133] Human Rights Watch telephone interview with the IDF Spokesperson, April 16, 1996.

ninety-minute period that morning.[134]   In the village of Zawtar al-Gharbiyeh, a father of eleven children said that over the years "every house in this village has been shelled, sniped at, or had people killed or injured." He recalled that three shells fell around his own house at 3:00 p.m. on October 20, 1994. One landed on the street in front of the house, one in front of the veranda, and the third at the rear of the house. Fortunately, no one was physically injured in that attack.[135]

In another attack, on the morning of June 17, 1995, Muhammad Tabaja, an elderly farmer in Kafr Tibnit, was killed when shells fell on agricultural land where he was working. According to his nephew, Ghassan Tabaja (quoted above), a Lebanese policeman:

> At about 6:15 in the morning, my uncle went to his farm as usual to pick seeds. There was an operation by the resistance nearby. At 7:30 exactly, there was one large explosion. Then, minutes later, the Israelis started shelling hard at and around the village [from their position at Ali Taher], and firing with machine guns everywhere. There was shelling everywhere. All of us ran to our houses, looking for shelter. It lasted for one hour. I was at my uncle's house as a car passed by very fast. It was a relative of mine, who signalled us to follow in our car. We went to the government hospital. It was then that I found out that my uncle was in that car. He was mutilated, his back was open and it was empty inside, and his right leg was missing.

The nephew said that three shells had landed where his uncle had been working. "The first one hit my uncle. Twenty sheep and goats were killed as well."

A month earlier, May 30, 1995, Amal Maruneh, a girl of twelve, was killed while her friend Maisa Ismail, also twelve, was seriously injured (her left leg had to be amputated above the knee) in the shelling of Shaqra, close to the Israeli-occupied area. According to Maisa's mother:

---

[134] Human Rights Watch interview, Kafr Tibnit, August 23, 1995. Unexploded munitions are a problem in southern Lebanon, where shells from the current conflict and the civil war continue to endanger civilians. In December 1995, five Lebanese children were wounded when an old antitank shell they were playing with exploded. "Old war bomb wounds five children in south Lebanon," Reuters, December 28, 1995.

[135] Human Rights Watch interview, Zawtar al-Gharbiyeh, August 23, 1995.

> There were no [military] operations going on. It was 6:30 or
> 7:00 at night. We were sitting here, in the living room. My sons
> were drinking tea on the roof and the children were playing
> outside the house. One of Maisa's friends asked her if she
> wanted to go to the husseiniya [a religious gathering place] and
> she said no.[136]

Maisa stayed with her mother in the house, along with her friend Amal. According
to the mother:

> Right after that, the first shell fell. I saw a lot of smoke and went
> downstairs. I saw that Amal was dead. I did not know then that
> my daughter had been struck as well. I was about to run out of
> the house when the second shell came down. Then I saw that
> my daughter had been injured. We started screaming for cars to
> come, but everyone was at the husseiniya.

Earlier that month, May 4, one civilian, Hassan 'Ali Karaki, was
reportedly killed during an IDF/SLA shelling of Jarju', and two, Rida' Ibrahim
Darwish, fifty-five, and his wife Latifah Darwish, were injured.[137] Hizballah
responded by firing five rockets at the town of Kiryat Shemona in northern Israel,
slightly wounding three civilians. This attack was described as "a first warning"
to Israel that the resistance was still willing to retaliate against Israeli civilians
when Lebanese civilians were hit.[138]

Civilian areas in south Lebanon sometimes come under indiscriminate fire
within minutes of attacks by Lebanese guerrillas on Israeli or SLA military targets
inside the security zone. For example, at 5:30 a.m. on February 19, 1995,
Hizballah guerrillas launched a coordinated attack, with rockets, mortars and

---

[136] Human Rights Watch interview, Shaqra, August 18, 1995. A husseiniya is a
gathering place for Shi'a Muslims where they hold prayer meetings and, on the anniversary
of the death of Imam Husein, celebrate al-'ashoura.

[137] "Casualties From Israeli Shelling Reported," Radio Lebanon, in FBIS-NES-95-
087, May 5, 1995, p. 26.

[138] "Hizballah Calls Katyusha Attack 'First Warning,'" Voice of Lebanon, May
5, 1995, in FBIS-NES-95-088, May 8, 1995, p. 36.

machine guns, on twelve SLA and IDF positions in the occupied area.[139]
Retaliation was swift, according to testimony taken by Human Rights Watch,
resulting in two civilian deaths in the village of Kafr Ruman: Khaled Midlij, thirty-
seven and a father of six, and Lana Abu Zeid, twenty-three, a university student,
were killed in a shelling barrage.[140] Mr. Midlij's wife said that there had been no
military activity by guerrilla forces in the village prior to the attack: "They started
shelling at about 5:30 in the morning, all throughout the village. Our house was
hit at about 7:00. The first shell struck the wall, the second landed on the road
outside the house, and the third landed on our verandah." She said the shells
followed closely upon one another: "We didn't have a chance to run away."
Shrapnel from the last shell came into the house through the window above the
verandah, killing Mr. Midlij and injuring three of his children.[141] Lana Abu Zeid,
who was visiting the village from Beirut to attend the funeral of a relative, died
when two shells exploded at the rear of the house where she was staying. Ms. Abu
Zeid's mother, Samira Salameh, forty-two, was injured in the attack.[142] Hospital
records indicate that Ms. Salameh was brought into the emergency room at 8:10 on
February 19, semi-conscious and in shock, with "a large foreign body in her lower
right abdomen."[143]

Residents of Kafr Ruman, interviewed in August 1995, said that the
shelling had been more frequent in 1994 than in 1995, but that the sporadic nature
of the shelling of the village in 1995 had brought uncertainty and tension rather
than relief. "Today, you are not sure whether you will be living tomorrow," one
resident said. "Two days ago, we were sleeping and they started shelling at about
11:30 at night. It lasted for four or five hours, then they started firing with machine

---

[139] *Mideast Mirror*, February 20, 1995. Hizballah said that the attacks were
intended to commemorate the assassinations of Sheikh Ragheb Harb on February 16, 1984,
and Sheikh Abbas Musawi on February 16, 1992, by Israeli forces. Ibid.

[140] "Israelis, Hizballah Inflict Casualties," Voice of Lebanon, February 19, 1995,
in FBIS-NES-95-034, February 21, 1995, p. 74; and Human Rights Watch interviews, Kafr
Ruman, August 21, 1995.

[141] Human Rights Watch interview, Kafr Ruman, August 21, 1995.

[142] Human Rights Watch interview with relatives, Kafr Ruman, August 21, 1995.

[143] Records of the Hospital of the Secours Populaire Libanais in Nabatiyeh,
reviewed by Human Rights Watch.

guns at houses, trees, and cars."[144]   Residents also said that there are no warning signs to indicate when shelling will begin. On October 22, 1995, machine gun fire from Israeli forces injured five-year-old Husein Alloush, also in Kafr Ruman, in the head. According to Reuters, bullets "rained down on the village" in retaliation for a guerrilla attack on IDF positions in the occupied area.[145] In two separate attacks on the village of Nabatiyeh al-Fowqa, seven civilians were killed and seven others injured by tank-fired antipersonnel shells that spread thousands of steel darts, called flechettes, over a wide area.[146]

Other attacks against civilians in southern Lebanon have been carried out by the Israeli Air Force (IAF). On August 4, 1994, at approximately 5:00 p.m., in the village of Deir al-Zahrani, a three-story house, home to seventeen people in four families, was hit by a rocket fired by an Israeli aircraft. Six residents were killed in the attack, while others were injured. The house, located in a residential area, was the only building in the village that was hit. Residents said that first a missile was fired at a nearby mountain and then, less than fifteen minutes later, the house was struck. "There was nothing military near the house," one resident said, as neighbors nodded in agreement. "They never hit this area before."[147] Residents said that about a month after the attack, another missile landed in the village at 9:00 in the evening, causing some damage but no injuries.

In addition to civilian casualties, the damage done by the fighting in southern Lebanon imposes an enormous financial burden on civilians of the region. The widow of Khaled Midlij in Kafr Ruman said that it cost $2,000 to repair the

---

[144] Human Rights Watch interview, Kafr Ruman, August 21, 1995.

[145] Reuters, October 22, 1995.

[146] See the section on flechettes in Chapter VI for a more detailed account of these two attacks.

[147] Human Rights Watch interviews, Deir al-Zahrani, August 17, 1995. Three children, two women and one man were killed. The victims were: Ghaleb Zawawi, 43, and two of his four children: Muhammad, 15, and Ali, 7 months; Hiyam Trabulsi, 23; Najah Trabulsi, 42, the wife of the owner of the house; and Husein Romani, 7. Israel apologized for this attack. The apology for the error, according to a government source, included " a calculation also that [Secretary of State Warren] Christopher, who was visiting shortly, would be able to say [to Arab leaders], 'Look, the Israelis apologized. They really did not intend for this to come out the way it did, and therefore the agreement stands.'" Israel claimed the cause of the error was under investigation. Reported by Caryle Murphy, "Timing a Key to Israeli Bomb Apology," *Washington Post*, August 6, 1994.

damage and construct the protective wall around the exterior of her home. This was an enormous investment for her. When asked if she considered leaving the village, she replied, "we [her family] have nowhere else to go."[148]

Hizballah is also responsible for indiscriminate attacks on civilian areas. On July 30, 1995, at least ten Lebanese civilians were wounded when a shell fired by Hizballah guerrillas hit the village of Rihan in the Israeli-occupied area.[149] On November 28, 1995, Hizballah forces fired at least twenty-four Katyusha rockets at the Israeli town of Kiryat Shemona, injuring eight people.[150]

Both parties continue to terrorize and harass civilians in contravention of international law. Threats of attacks from both the IDF/SLA and Hizballah, many of which never materialize, send terrorized people anxiously searching for shelter and cause much distress. Israel often mounts mock raids and breaks the sound barrier over southern Lebanon and Beirut. These attacks disrupt daily life and cause a constant state of anxiety. Intermittent and unannounced shelling and rocket attacks kill, maim and injure. There is little, if any, sense of security and the inhabitants of southern Lebanon and northern Israel must live in a world where their safety is based on the actions of others they cannot control. This is especially the case in southern Lebanon, where the inhabitants are unable to influence the actions of either Hizballah or the IDF/SLA. Article 51(2) of Protocol I provides in part: "Acts or threats of violence the primary purpose of which is to spread terror among the civilian population are prohibited." (See also the section on warnings in chapter 5 below).

---

[148] Human Rights Watch interview, Kafr Ruman, August 21, 1995. Shelling by the IDF/SLA in southern Lebanon has also caused foreign casualties. In 1995 the IDF killed one Nepalese soldier and wounded three others when shells fell on the Nepalese UNIFIL battalion based in the village of Yatar. ("Israeli Shelling Kills UNIFIL Soldier," Radio Lebanon, March 20, 1995, in FBIS-NES-95-053, March 20, 1995, p. 26). A Syrian worker was killed and three others wounded when the IDF shelled the town of Mashgharah in the Beqa', where the Syrian army maintains a military post. ("Syrian Said Killed in Israeli Shelling," AFP, March 23, 1995, in FBIS-NES-95-057, March 24, 1995, p. 43). Three Norwegian UNIFIL soldiers on foot patrol were lightly wounded by flechettes from Israeli tank shells in December 1995. ("U.N. troops hit by Israeli fire," *Washington Post*, December 10, 1995).

[149] "Guerrillas Kill Israeli Soldier in S. Lebanon," *Washington Post*, July 31, 1995.

[150] Serge Schmemann, "Lebanese Rebels Fire Rockets Over Border Into Northern Israel," *New York Times*, November 29, 1995.

In addition to incursions into Lebanese airspace and the occupation of the self-described "security zone," Israel has also, since February 1995, imposed a blockade on Lebanese territorial waters that exacts a heavy price on Lebanese fishermen. Attempts by fishermen to evade the blockade have been met with direct attacks by Israeli forces against the fishermen. The blockade was in apparent retaliation for what Israel claimed was a Lebanese army policy of harassment of residents of occupied southern Lebanon at checkpoints between Lebanese-controlled territory and the Israeli-occupied area.[151] The blockade was initially imposed on the coastline around Tyre on February 10, 1995 and then extended a few days later to Sidon. On February 21, the speaker of the Lebanese parliament, Nabih Berri, who is also the leader of the Amal movement, charged that Israel had notified the Lebanese army command that the blockade on Tyre would be lifted if the policy of searching cars crossing from Israeli-occupied Lebanon into Lebanon at army checkpoints were ended. Berri termed the offer "extortion," noted that one reason for the searches was fear of booby-trapped cars, and added: "It is our right to take all measures to shield our security and protect stability from any setback at the hands of the saboteur networks working for Israel."[152] On February 25, the blockade was further extended northwards to encompass the port of Damour, eighteen kilometers (eleven miles) south of Beirut. On March 2, Lebanese foreign minister Fares Bouez sent a letter of protest to U.N. Secretary-General Boutros Boutros-Ghali, claiming that the blockade had been extended north to the ports of Sarafand, Sidon and Damour the previous week, affecting 1,800 fishermen.[153]

Israel has enforced the blockade with vigor. For instance, on March 16, 1995, Israeli gunboats fired on fishermen off the coast of Tyre. On another occasion, March 27, an Israeli gunboat fired on fishermen fishing four kilometers off the coast of Sidon, forcing them to abandon valuable equipment.[154] In another confrontation, on May 9, Israeli gunboats chased thirteen fishing boats near the

---

[151] According to press reports, the restrictions were aimed at putting pressure on the Lebanese government "to ease [Lebanese Army] security checks at crossings into Israel's occupation zone in southern Lebanon." *New York Times*, March 3, 1995.

[152] *Mideast Mirror*, February 22, 1995.

[153] "Lebanon Asks UN To Halt Israeli Blockade," *New York Times*, March 3, 1995.

[154] "Gunboats Fire at Fishing Boats," Radio Free Lebanon, March 27, 1995, in FBIS-NES-95-058, March 27, 1995, p. 61.

Tyre shore and forced them to return to shore.[155] Tyre fishermen working within the one-kilometer zone have been harassed by Israeli gunboats that patrol the waters. "Three weeks ago, they started shooting at us," one fisherman told Human Rights Watch. "We were putting out our nets. They put a spotlight on us and started shooting without warning over our heads." He said that the Israeli boats were fifteen to twenty yards away. The fishermen left their nets and returned to shore. He said that in another incident, a bullet grazed the plastic hood of a fisherman's raingear, and another time an Israeli gunboat rammed a wooden fishing boat and damaged its side. Fishermen at the port showed Human Rights Watch a red plastic container riddled with bulletholes; such containers are used as buoys to mark the nets at sea. "Every time we leave the port, we feel danger," one fisherman said. "When they attack us, we cut the nets and try to escape."[156]

Farouq, a fisherman, claimed he had been fishing for twenty-five years. "Two months ago, they started to shoot at my boat at sunrise," he said. "There was no warning. They turned on their lights and started firing." He said that dozens of bullets were fired, but that his boat was not hit. "I turned around and came back. I am scared. I will go out for one day and then not go out for twenty days."[157] Other Tyre fishermen said that about 250 fishing boats leave the port daily between midnight and 2:00 a.m., and return at 6:00 or 7:00 in the morning. The one-kilometer restriction substantially affects their livelihood. "I go out every day," one fisherman said. "I used to bring back fifteen or twenty or thirty kilograms; now, I bring back only two kilograms."[158]

Harassment and detention of Lebanese fishermen continued during the six-month period from July 1995 to January 1996. According to a U.N. report:

> As before, Israeli naval vessels patrolled Lebanese territorial waters in the south and imposed restrictions on the local fishermen. At times, this involved firing at or near fishing boats and temporary detention of Lebanese fishermen. UNIFIL

---

[155] "'Enemy' Israeli Gunboats Chase Fishing Boats," Radio Free Lebanon, May 9, 1995, in FBIS-NES-95-090, May 10, 1995, p. 37.

[156] Human Rights Watch interviews, Tyre, August 24, 1995.

[157] Human Rights Watch interview, Tyre, August 24, 1995.

[158] Human Rights Watch interview, Tyre, August 24, 1995.

intervened with the Israeli authorities repeatedly for the release of those detained.[159]

According to witnesses, IDF/SLA troops have also fired shots at farmers working their fields in villages close to the front line, and have fired phosphorus shells or other incendiaries, such as tracer rounds and smoke grenades, at these fields, setting them on fire, in efforts to clear the suspect population from the region, halt economic activity there, and enforce an unofficial no-man's land between the two sides. A farmer in Zawtar al-Sharqiyeh told Human Rights Watch: "The [Litani] river is two kilometers away from [our] fields. They will not let anyone near the river. They say it is a military area."[160] Farmers wanting to till their land or harvest their crops have been fired at. "We cannot go into the fields because they shoot at us," one Shaqra resident told Human Rights Watch. Farmers said that they are demanding compensation from the Lebanese government for the substantial agricultural losses they have incurred. They complain that attacks have wiped out harvests of wheat, other grains, and olives. "People have had to take UNIFIL soldiers with them to harvest olives," one resident said.[161] UNIFIL confirmed this: "We go with an armored personnel carrier, raise the U.N. flag, and stay with them while they harvest," a spokesman said.[162] Shaqra residents said that, in the case of their village, the shelling comes mainly from the Israeli military position at Hula.

Such tactics have had an impact over the last eleven years, forcing residents who depend heavily on agriculture for their livelihoods to leave. "The Israelis are destroying houses, burning crops, forcing civilians to leave. Every year, they burn the same land here," the farmer in Zawtar al-Sharqiyeh, whose family owns six to seven dunums of land, said.[163] He added that the now-forbidden agricultural lands used to yield about US$200,000 annually in crops for

---

[159] United Nations Security Council, *Report of the Secretary General on the United Nations Interim Force in Lebanon*, par. 5.

[160] Human Rights Watch interview, Zawtar al-Sharqiyeh, August 23, 1995. The same witness is quoted in the section on the use of phosphorus in chapter 6 below.

[161] Human Rights Watch interview, Shaqra, August 18, 1995.

[162] Human Rights Watch interview, Tyre, August 29, 1995.

[163] A dunum equals approximately 900 square meters.

thefamilies that farmed there, and that he was losing about $5,000 to $6,000 a year in income that he would normally have received from the harvest of olives and tobacco. "About a third of the families in the village have left in ten years," he said. "Originally there were 300 families. Now there are 200."[164] In neighboring Zawtar al-Gharbiyeh, a resident who was born in the village in 1935 said that he refuses to leave. But he added that for the last ten years his family has forfeited the income from its twenty dunums of agricultural land in the "forbidden" zone planted with olive, fig, and orange trees, and *huboub* [grains]. He said that of 300 families with agricultural land in the "forbidden" area, some fifty-five have left the village.[165] Residents of Shaqra village also told Human Rights Watch that the burning of agricultural land had forced many families, dependent on agriculture, to leave the area.[166]

Operation Grapes of Wrath

In April 1996, the de facto cease-fire that had ended the July 1993 fighting broke down under the weight of cumulative violations by both sides of the agreement not to target the adversary's civilian population. Between March 4 and April 10, five weeks of attacks and reprisals had killed seven Israeli soldiers, three Lebanese civilians and at least one Hizballah fighter.[167] The tally of injured was sixteen Israeli soldiers, seven Lebanese civilians, and six Israeli civilians. The attacks came during the Israeli election campaign and brought extra pressure on the Labor Party-led coalition government to respond militarily against Hizballah without regard for the limitations implicit in the July 1993 understandings. On April 9, Israel's deputy defense minister, Ori Orr, warned Lebanese civilians, referring to the July 1993 understandings: "It is clear that these rules of the game are not good and cannot remain and it is necessary that the Lebanese population living north of the security zone will live under more fear than it lives today,"[168]

---

[164] Human Rights Watch interview, Zawtar al-Sharqiyeh, August 23, 1995.

[165] Human Rights Watch interview, Zawtar al-Gharbiyeh, August 23, 1995.

[166] Human Rights Watch interviews, Shaqra, August 18, 1995.

[167] "Lebanon: Main Events in Recent Hizbollah-Israel Violence," Reuters, April 11, 1996.

[168] Shlomi Afriat, "Israel vows retaliation for Lebanon rocket attacks." Reuters, April 9, 1996.

while Maj.-Gen. Amiram Levine declared: "[T]he residents in south Lebanon who are under the responsibility of Hizbullah will be hit harder, and the Hizbullah will be hit harder, and we will find the way to act correctly and quickly."[169] Within forty-eight hours, Israel launched what it referred to as "Operation Grapes of Wrath."

On April 11, Israel launched air and artillery attacks against what it claimed were Hizballah military and infrastructural targets, including a helicopter gunship attack on a building housing the Hizballah consultative council, or *shura*, in a southern Beirut suburb.[170] These attacks killed three Lebanese civilians and one Lebanese soldier. Following renewed Hizballah Katyusha attacks on northern Israel, Israel issued warnings, via the SLA radio station, to civilians in forty-four villages and towns in southern Lebanon, including the city of Nabatiyeh, to leave their homes by 2:30 p.m. the next day, April 12.[171] U.N. sources in southern Lebanon reported that the attacks that commenced around 4:30 p.m. were heavier and less discriminating than the attacks with laser-guided weapons on Thursday.[172] Attacks also continued against targets in Beirut and elsewhere, and one Syrian soldier was killed and seven wounded in an attack on a highway military post near Beirut's international airport.[173]

The next day, April 13, Israeli warships initiated a blockade against Beirut, Sidon and Tyre, Lebanon's chief ports of entry. The same day, an Israeli helicopter gunship rocketed an ambulance carrying fleeing civilians near Tyre, killing two women and four children and bringing the death toll to at least twenty-

---

[169] Derek Brown, "Lebanon accord in jeopardy," *The Guardian* (London), April 10, 1996.

[170] Israel claims to have hit the *shura* building. A Reuters dispatch of April 11 ("Four Dead in Israeli Attacks on Lebanon") said rather that "Israeli rockets destroyed a two-storey building next to the building of the Shura...." A Reuters dispatch the next day, April 12 ("Israel Arch Foe Hizbollah—Tough Nut to Crack") also reported that the Council building "escaped a direct hit."

[171] "Israel Steps Up Lebanese Attacks," *Washington Post*, April 13, 1996, p. A23.

[172] Ibid.

[173] Ibid.

one people, by the estimate of Lebanese journalists.[174]   Israeli government spokesman Uri Dromi declared that "We gave the residents advance warning to clear out so as not to get hurt. All those who remain there, do so at their own risk because we assume they're connected with Hizbollah."[175] On April 14, an army spokesman said: "Anyone remaining in Tyre or these forty villages [which had been named in warnings]...is solely responsible for endangering his life."[176]

By Monday, April 15, Israeli/SLA warnings to flee had been extended to a total of eighty-six Lebanese communities. As in July 1993, such warnings were in part designed to provoke a major humanitarian crisis by internally displacing upwards of 400,000 Lebanese civilians. "Even if you tie me up and whip me, I'm not going to admit on-the-record that our policy is to force out civilians to put pressure on the Lebanese government," one Israeli official told the *Wall Street Journal*. "But let's just say we hope Lebanon understands the message."[177]

Meanwhile, Hizballah reprisals, in the form of Katyusha salvos into northern Israel, continued without respite. On Sunday, April 14, Israel attacked a electric power station in Jumhour, just outside Beirut, and on Monday, April 15,

---

[174] "Israel Expands Retaliation on Lebanon," *Washington Post*, April 14, 1996, pp. A1, A26. A27. This dispatch also cites the eyewitness account of the ambulance attack by Reuters correspondent Najla Abu Jahjah. Lt.-Gen. Amnon Shahak, Israel's chief of general staff, said that "the ambulance hit in Tyre was to the best of our knowledge transporting a Hezbollah terrorist from one Hezbollah position in the area of Tyre to another." He added that "when all the details will be known, it will be conclusively proven that the target was Hezbollah terrorists using the ambulance for their own needs." According to Abu Jahjah, the vehicle was marked with the logo of the Islamic Scouts Association, an offshoot of Amal, a rival Shi`a group to Hizballah. Israel has yet to provide the evidence it claims to have for its assertion.

In an interview published in the *Washington Post* on April 17 ("Rocket Shatters a Family," p. A29), Abbas Jihah, the driver, whose wife and three daughters were among those killed, said "I believe in God and everything, but there's no way I would be involved with Hizbollah." He claimed that he "was trying to help needy people and get my family out of danger. If I were Hizballah, I would not have been in the ambulance carrying bread or trying to save my family. It would have been too dangerous." An interview with Jihah also appeared in the *Los Angeles Times* on the same day.

[175] "Israel Says Checking Report on Ambulance Attack," Reuters, April 13, 1996.

[176] "Israel Extends Deadline for Tyre Evacuation," Reuters, April 14, 1996.

[177] "Lebanese Civilians Become Israel's Pawns," *Wall Street Journal*, April 16, 1996, p. A11.

struck a power station in Bsaleem in the eastern part of Beirut, asserting that the attacks were in response to an earlier Hizballah rocket attack. An Israeli army spokesman characterized the Hizballah attack, which reportedly cut an electric cable to a synagogue in Kiryat Shemona, as an attack on "electrical infrastructure in northern Israel."[178]

On April 18, an Israeli strike on a village near Nabatiyeh destroyed a building, killing a woman, her seven children and a cousin. A few hours later, Israeli artillery shells hit a makeshift refugee compound at a UNIFIL post in Qana, some ten kilometers south of Tyre, killing more than 100 displaced civilians who had fled their homes.

Prior to the carnage on April 18, the death toll and destruction had been mounting, along with evidence that Israeli forces were carrying out indiscriminate and disproportionate attacks against civilians in what had become virtual "free-fire" zones across large swaths of the south. The *Jerusalem Post* reported the "strong protest" that the U.N. had lodged with the IDF when "planes had dropped bombs in front of a clearly marked two-vehicle U.N. convoy trying to take essential items to refugees taking shelter in and around U.N. positions."[179] The onslaught in the area southeast of Tyre was particularly ferocious. On April 15, over 700 shells and 30 air-to-surface missiles and bombs poured down in a four-hour period, the U.N. said.[180] Journalists were unable to investigate the destruction in villages near Tyre "because of the intense bombing and shelling," Reuters reported on April 16.[181] Reuters correspondent Haitham Haddadin filed a dispatch from Tyre that day, extensively quoting residents who had fled nearby villages. "It's random shelling....They are sparing nothing. They are hitting homes and fields and civilians," one said. Up to one hundred shells, bombs and rockets were landing

---

[178] "If It's Lights Out for Israeli Synagogue, Beirut Must Go Dark Too," *Washington Post*, April 16, 1996, p. A11. The article, datelined Kiryat Shemona, noted that between Thursday, April 11, and Monday, April 15, some 140 Katyushas had fallen on Israel, while Israel had "fired more than 5,000 rounds of artillery into Lebanon and flown many hundreds of bombing sorties."

[179] David Rudge, "Two wounded in Katyusha attacks," *The Jerusalem Post*, April 18, 1996.

[180] "Israel Hits Lebanon Again, US Offers Peace Plan," Reuters, April 16, 1996, citing UNIFIL sources.

[181] Ibid.

every hour in the village of Mansouri, a resident claimed, noting that "about 20 big guns" overlooking the village were "firing incredibly fast."[182]

These attacks, and the stated positions that accompanied them, put Israel in violation of the laws of war, which impose upon the attacker the duty to discriminate at all times between civilians and military targets. Civilians who cannot or will not flee areas that an attacker has ordered evacuated—such as the elderly, the infirm, and women with newborn children—do not automatically lose their protection under the laws of war. Nor can the attacker simply assume that those left behind are combatants and therefore subject to attack as military targets. These long-recognized principles of civilian immunity are codified in the Geneva Conventions, and subsequent restatements of customary international humanitarian law, in compellingly clear terms.

The death toll from the April 18 attack on the peacekeeping base at Qana stood at 102 civilians as of April 24. According to *The Independent*, five of the shells that landed at the base on the afternoon of April 18 were believed to be 155mm shells fired by U.S.-made M-109 self-propelled howitzers.[183] In a later report, citing the U.N., *The Independent* stated that six 155mm shells landed within the UNIFIL compound and between fifty and sixty shells landed in Qana on April 18. "According to U.N. sources in Lebanon, the Israeli shells were fitted with M732 radar fuses, which detonate them at [seven meters] off the ground, the most lethal possible height, blasting fragments downwards to amputate, maim and kill."[184]

Following the attack, Lt.-Gen. Amnon Shahak, Israel's chief of staff, defended the shelling by dismissing long-established, internationally accepted laws of war. "I don't see any mistake in judgment....We fought Hizballah there [in Qana], and when they fire on us, we will fire at them to defend ourselves....I don't know any other rules of the game, either for the army or for civilians," he said at a press conference in Tel Aviv on April 18.[185]

---

[182] Haitham Haddadin, "Israeli Blitz Spares Nothing," Reuters, April 16, 1996.

[183] Christopher Bellamy, "Lebanon: Artillery 'Cock-Up' Costs Scores of Lebanese Lives," *The Independent*, April 19, 1996.

[184] Christopher Bellamy, "Israel: Artillery Bombardment 'Defied Orders,'" *The Independent*, April 23, 1996.

[185] "Israeli Army Chief Says UN Forewarned of Shelling," Reuters, April 18, 1996.

Gen. Shahak was referring to the provocation that brought on the protracted Israeli response. A U.N. spokeswoman had confirmed that, fifteen minutes before the attack, Hizballah guerrillas had fired mortars and Katyusha rockets from a position some three hundred meters from the base.[186] Both the U.S. and Israel accused Hizballah of "shielding"—the use of civilians as a cover for military activities, which is a breach of the laws of war. "Hizballah [is] using civilians as cover. That's a despicable thing to do, an evil thing," the U.S. State Department spokesperson said.[187] Prime Minister Peres cited shielding to shift blame for the massacre to Hizballah. "They used them as a shield, they used the U.N. as a shield—the U.N. admitted it," he said on April 18.[188]

Any acts of shielding committed by Hizballah violate humanitarian law. They do not, however, give Israel license to fire indiscriminately into a wide are that includes a U.N. base and concentrations of civilians. The Geneva-based International Committee of the Red Cross, which issues press releases only sparingly while international armed conflicts are raging, issued a strongly worded statement on April 19, in which it "firmly condemned" the Israeli shelling at Qana, and noted the "absolute ban" on indiscriminate attacks under the laws of war. The ICRC stated that Israeli orders for the evacuation of large areas of south Lebanon did not "exempt Israel from the obligation to respect the civilians still on the spot." The ICRC also noted the Israeli orders to evacuate "in this case [were] contrary to international humanitarian law."[189]

---

[186] U.N. spokeswoman Sylvana Foa at the United Nations in New York said that the commander of UNIFIL "has confirmed to us that Hizbollah forces, about fifteen minutes before the Israeli shelling, fired two Katyushas and eight mortars from a position about 300 meters from the Fijian headquarters." "United Nations: Hizbollah Fired From Near U.N. Post Hit by Israel," Reuters, April 18, 1996.

[187] Steven Erlanger, "Christopher Sees Syria Chief in Bid on Lebanon Truce," *The New York Times,* April 21, 1996, quoting State Department spokesman Nicholas Burns.

[188] Serge Schmemann, "Voicing Regret, Israeli Leader Offers a Cease-Fire," *The New York Times,* April 19, 1996. In a speech to the Israeli Knesset on April 22, Peres declared: "The terrible tragedy of Kafr Kana and the suffering of Lebanon in general are entirely the fault of the terrorist organizations, first and foremost, of Hizbullah." Information Division, Israel Foreign Ministry, "Address by Prime Minister Shimon Peres to the Knesset on the IDF Operations in Lebanon," April 22, 1996.

[189] "ICRC Condemns Shelling of Civilians in Southern Lebanon," Communication to the press no. 96/14, April 19, 1996.

Article 58(b) of Protocol 1 instructs parties to a conflict to "avoid locating military objectives within or near densely populated areas." The protocol does not specify the precise distance where a military target must be located in order not to be "near" a densely populated area. Nor does the protocol indicate proper locations for fixed military targets—bases, permanent artillery installations, command and control centers, etc.—compared to highly mobile military targets, such as Katyusha launchers, that can quickly be moved or abandoned after firing.[190]

Even if Hizballah was guilty of shielding its military operations in Qana on April 18, the laws of war did not give Israeli forces unlimited license to attack indiscriminately the general area from which the guerrillas fired mortars and Katyushas. The Israeli assault on the base and its environs must be judged against two key legal requirements. Parties to an armed conflict must refrain from indiscriminate attacks (defined as operations that are not directed at a specific military objective but that strike military targets and civilian without distinction), and from disproportionate attacks (those in which the military advantage to be

---

[190] Article 51(7) of Protocol 1 defines shielding as follows: "The presence or movements of the civilian population or individual civilians shall not be used to render certain points or areas immune from military operations, in particular in attempts to shield military objectives from attacks or to shield, favour or impede military operations. The Parties to the conflict shall not direct the movement of the civilian population or individual civilians in order to attempt to shield military objectives from attacks or to shield military operations." One authoritative commentary on Protocol 1 cites as an example of shielding "cases in which civilian refugees are herded down a road either as a shield for a moving column of combatants, or to impede the movement of the adversary's columns." Other examples would include placement of military communications or command and control equipment inside a clearly marked civilian air raid shelter (this was the justification offered by the U.S. for its attack on the al-'Ameriyeh air raid shelter in Baghdad on February 13, 1991 that claimed the lives of 204 civilians. See Middle East Watch, *Needless Deaths in the Gulf War: Civilian Casualties During the Air Campaign and Violations of the Laws of War* (New York: Human Rights Watch, 1991), pp. 128-147), or locating combatants inside hospitals or other buildings that are protected from attack under the laws of war (Iraq used this to justify its destruction of historic Shi'a religious shrines in Najaf and Karbala in southern Iraq during the 1991 post-Operation Desert Storm uprising. See Middle East Watch, "Endless Torment: The 1991 Uprising in Iraq and Its Aftermath" (New York: Human Rights Watch, 1992), pp. 51-56). Hizballah certainly did not "direct" the civilians to the U.N. base. They had fled their villages southeast of Tyre because of shelling and bombing by Israeli forces. U.N. personnel had earlier evacuated many of them from their homes, and housed them at the base for humanitarian reasons. In this case the prohibition against "locating military objectives within or near densely populated areas" is the more relevant one.

gained is outweighed by excessive collateral damage to civilians). Israel violated these basic principles of the laws of war when it attacked the U.N. base and its environs.

Prime Minister Shimon Peres claimed that "We did not know that several hundred people were concentrated in that camp. It came to us as a bitter surprise."[191] The claim itself is questionable. By the IDF's own account, its forces can track the movement of individual guerrillas after the firing of Katyusha rockets.[192] Given Israel's air reconnaissance over south Lebanon during Operation Grapes of Wrath, it is difficult to imagine that the presence of over 800 civilians at a U.N. base went unnoticed.

Even if Israel did not know that civilians were housed there, its assault was nonetheless a violation of the laws of war. The base itself, with 200 Fijian peacekeepers, was not a legitimate military target. British journalist Robert Fisk, who was traveling nearby with a U.N. humanitarian convoy at the time of the attack, heard the first big guns fire into Qana just after 2 p.m. Then he heard, at 2:10 p.m., an anxious Fijian soldier report on the radio: "Our headquarters are being shelled." Two minutes later, someone from the U.N. operations headquarters in Naqqoura came on the air with these words: "We are contacting the IDF." The Fijian came back on the line, shouting: "Do you understand? They are firing on us now. The headquarters is hit." Fisk noted the time, 2:20 pm, and wrote: "There had been six incoming rounds, then more. The guns I had heard were firing a shell every five seconds. A Lebanese U.N. liaison man came on the line from the burning...headquarters. 'People are dying here. We need help.'"[193] The protracted Israeli fire at the clearly-marked base and its environs is a classic example of an indiscriminate attack under the laws of war, which forbid treating an entire area as a military target. The breach is signficant because throughout Operation Grapes of Wrath Israel widely publicized its capacity to execute surgical strikes against Hizballah.

Hours before the attack on Qana, Israeli fighter-bombers rocketed a two-story home in the southern village of Nabatiyeh al-Fowqa, killing a mother, her

---

[191] Serge Schmemann, "Voicing Regret, Israeli Leader Offers a Cease-Fire," *The New York Times,* April 19, 1996.

[192] Note the Israeli claims cited below with regard to the IDF attack on civilian homes in Nabatiyeh al-Fowqa earlier the same day.

[193] Robert Fisk, "Desperate Voices Go Unheard As Shells Rain Down," *The Independent*, April 19, 1996.

new-born child, six of her other children, and a relative. According to press reports, another house, thirty meters away, was also hit, injuring four children and their parents.[194] Israeli Prime Minister Shimon Peres declared: "We don't fire at buildings for no reason. We only hit at those buildings from which Katyushas were fired....But naturally Nabatiyeh was supposed to be vacant."[195] The IDF itself did not claim that Katyushas had been fired from the Nabatiyeh houses. Neither did it provide evidence to support its claim that guerrillas ran to these houses after attacking an IDF post.[196] In either case, the civilians who remained in Nabatiyeh al-Fowqa had not forfeited protection under the laws of war, as the IDF has the duty to exercise discretion when attacking civilian houses to avoid civilian casualties excessive of the anticipated military advantage.

As this report went to press (April 25) Israeli attacks and Hizballah reprisals were well into their fifteenth day, already exceeding the duration of the war of July 1993. The casualty toll of Operation Grapes of Wrath had reached about 150 Lebanese killed and some 300 wounded, almost all of them civilians. Casualties on the Israeli side were reported by the IDF to be twenty-six injured.[197]

---

[194] Maher Chmaytelli, "Mother, Eight Children Die as Israeli Air Raid Destroys Home," Agence France Presse, April 18, 1996.

[195] Serge Schmemann, "Voicing Regret, Israeli Leader Offers a Cease-Fire," *The New York Times,* April 19, 1996. In a speech to the Israeli Knesset on April 22, Peres declared: "The terrible tragedy of Kafr Kana and the suffering of Lebanon in general are entirely the fault of the terrorist organizations, first and foremost, of Hizbullah." Information Division, Israel Foreign Ministry, "Address by Prime Minister Shimon Peres to the Knesset on the IDF Operations in Lebanon," April 22, 1996.

[196] The text of the IDF spokesman's statement, dated April 18, 1996, was as follows: "This morning (Thursday), 18 April 1996, Hizballah terrorists attacked an IDF post at Ali Taher range, in the central sector of south Lebanon. Immediately after the operation, terrorists fled to the home of a Hizballah activist on outskirts of Nabatiya, south Lebanon. IAF helicopters sent to scene were fired upon by anti-aircraft fire from the area around the house to which the terrorists fled. IAF planes fired at and hit the house. IDF again warns community residents to evacuate homes to avoid harm, especially while Hizballah continues to use civilians homes to operate, hide and shoot into Galilee communities and at our forces."

[197] The Israeli figure of thirty-one injured includes five treated for shock, a category that is not used when reporting Lebanese casualties. Information Division, Israel Foreign Ministry, Jerusalem, April 21, 1996.

The BBC World Service reported on April 25 that Israeli forces had destroyed sections of roads and bridges in order to impede Lebanese from attending a mass memorial gathering for those killed in Qana.

V. OPERATION ACCOUNTABILITY / THE SEVEN-DAY WAR

Operation Accountability was a week-long Israeli military operation in July 1993 that constituted a massive escalation in the fighting in southern Lebanon; people there refer to it as the Seven-Day War.[198] According to UNIFIL sources, during the operation the IDF fired some 22,000 artillery rounds and 1,000 air-to-surface rockets against villages in the south of Lebanon, in addition to shells fired at the western Beq'a.[199] On one day alone, Monday, July 27, 1993, the IDF, by its own reckoning, fired 5,000 shells into southern Lebanon.[200] That same week, Israeli officials claim, Hizballah fired 151 Katyusha rockets into northern Israel and a further 122 into the Israeli-occupied area in southern Lebanon.[201] According to Lebanese prime minister Rafiq Hariri, one Lebanese soldier, eight Hizballah fighters and 118 Lebanese civilians were killed, while some 500 Lebanese civilians sustained injuries.[202] In Israel, two civilians were reported killed and twenty-four were injured.[203]

During the operation, the safety of civilians was deliberately manipulated by both sides to achieve their respective strategic goals. A primary declared goal of the Israeli operation was to drive Lebanese civilians north to Beirut and thereby pressure the Lebanese government to crack down on Hizballah, while punishing the villagers of southern Lebanon for allowing guerrillas to operate in the region. Likewise, Hizballah fired large numbers of Katyusha rockets at Israeli towns in order to cause civilian casualties and force the Israeli government to call off the

---

[198] The Israeli name of the operation has also been translated as "Operation Settling Accounts." Both versions are correct translations of the Hebrew "Din ve Kheshbon." It remains unclear which of the two meanings the operation's authors intended.

[199] "State Radio Updates Situation," Radio Lebanon, July 30, 1993, in FBIS-NES-93-145, July 30, 1993, p. 46.

[200] "Baraq: Lebanon Operation 'Successful So Far,'" Qol Yisra'el, July 28, 1993, in FBIS-NES-93-143, July 28, 1993, p. 20.

[201] Col. Ahaz Ben-Ari, head of the IDF's international law branch, in a communication to Human Rights Watch, May 18, 1994.

[202] David Hoffman, "Israel Halts Bombardment of Lebanon."

[203] Col. Ahaz Ben-Ari, head of the IDF's international law branch, in a communication to Human Rights Watch, May 18, 1994.

attack. Both sides were well aware that these actions were explicit violations of international humanitarian law.

Escalation

On July 8, 1993, more than two weeks before Operation Accountability, an ambush against an IDF patrol in the Israeli-occupied area left two Israeli soldiers dead and three injured. The Popular Front for the Liberation of Palestine-General Command (PFLP-GC), a small Palestinian faction based in Damascus, claimed responsibility for the attack.[204] The next day, July 9, Israel retaliated by attacking a PFLP-GC base near Na'meh, south of Beirut, with helicopters, and shelling the fields around villages in the Iqlim al-Tuffah (Apple Region), which is generally considered a stronghold of Hizballah fighters.[205] Later that same day, Hizballah commandos carried out an attack against a joint IDF/SLA post near Sujud in the IDF/SLA-controlled part of the Iqlim al-Tuffah, killing an additional three Israeli soldiers and injuring two.[206] This was the highest Israeli military casualty toll in southern Lebanon in years, and prompted a heated discussion in Israel about the IDF's role in southern Lebanon.

The Israeli response soon followed. On the morning of July 10, 1993, the Hizballah radio station reported that IDF/SLA forces had conducted a "brutal shelling" of villages in the Iqlim al-Tuffah and that homes had been hit in the assault. In retaliation for this attack, Hizballah claimed, it had fired "24 large-caliber rockets" at IDF/SLA positions in the occupied border zone.[207]

After this initial exchange, a tense calm prevailed as a war of words broke out. On July 11, Israeli Prime Minister Yitzhak Rabin was quoted as saying he had

---

[204] "Israeli Soldiers Reported Killed in Bomb Attack," AFP, July 8, 1993, in FBIS-NES-93-129, July, 8 1993, p. 31.

[205] "Raid on Jibril 'Terrorist' Base," Qol Yisra'el, and "'Violent' Israeli Shelling," Voice of the Mountain, July 9, 1993, both in FBIS-NES-93-129, July 9, 1993, pp. 28-29.

[206] "Three Dead, Five Wounded," Israel Television Network, July 12, 1993, in FBIS-NES-93-131, July 12, 1993, p. 45.

[207] "Hizballah Radio Reports Resistance on 'Maximum Alert,'" Voice of the Oppressed, in FBIS-NES-93-131, July 12, 1993, pp. 45-46. There were also unconfirmed reports of the use of phosphorus shells by Israel on July 10, and the firing of rockets at targets in the occupied border zone and inside Israel by Islamic Jihad-Beit al-Maqdis, a small Palestinian group, "Phosphorous Bombs Reported Fired at Jabal al-Rayhan," Radio Free Lebanon, July 10, in FBIS-NES-93-131, July 12, 1993, p. 46.

directed the IDF to prepare for a response, and military sources suggested that a "sharp Israeli reaction" might be possible.[208] More unabashedly, SLA commander Antoine Lahd said the next day on an Israeli radio station:

> I believe that retaliation this time will be harsh, and that *the people in the north of the security strip, as well as Lebanon*, will pay a price for this. It will not only be Hizballah, Ahmad Jibril's organization, or some organizations with ulterior motives that will pay a price this time.[209]

In a similar vein, and apparently in response, a senior Hizballah official was quoted the next day as warning Israel "against committing any foolish action, because we are ready to open the whole front and to cross all the political and geographic borders," a veiled reference to Katyusha attacks across the frontier.[210] From July 11 on, Israeli troop movements were observed in the Israeli-occupied area, and the media reported that the IDF was bringing tanks and artillery batteries across the border from Israel.[211]

The threats from both sides escalated over the next few days, accompanied by minor skirmishes that kept the embers of war glowing. On July 14, an Israeli "senior defense establishment source" told IDF radio that "Israel reserves the right to act against any element that acts against it, including Iran, Syria, Lebanon, *the Lebanese population*, and the terrorist organizations themselves."[212] The next day,

---

[208] "IDF Sources Urge 'Firm' Move in Lebanon," Davar, July 12, 1993, in FBIS-NES-93-131, July 12, 1993, p. 33. The Israeli coordinator of government activities in Lebanon, Uri Lubrani, stressed on July 9 that "what is happening on the ground now calls for a reconsideration of the situation." "Lubrani: Response to Terrorism Unrelated to Talks," Israel Television Network, July 9, 1993, in FBIS-NES-93-132, July 13, 1993, p. 36.

[209] "SLA Commander Warns of 'Harsh' Retaliation for Attacks," Qol Yisra'el, July 12, 1993, in FBIS-NES-93-132, July 13, 1993, p. 49 (emphasis added).

[210] "Hizballah Officer Denounces Envoy's Visit," Voice of the Oppressed, July 12, 1993, in FBIS-NES-93-131, July 12, 1993, p. 43.

[211] For example, "Resistance Notes Military Movement," Voice of Lebanon, July 12, 1993, in FBIS-NES-93-131, July 12, 1993, pp. 46-47.

[212] "Minister on Syrian Role in Situation in Lebanon," IDF Radio, July 14, 1993, in FBIS-NES-93-133, July 14, 1993, p. 26 (emphasis added).

the Israeli Air Force was reported to have attacked the village of Kafr Tibnit, damaging two homes and injuring a civilian, while guerrillas fired Katyushas at IDF/SLA positions in the occupied border zone.[213] On July 17, two Israeli soldiers were injured in an ambush by Palestinian commandos in the zone.

By July 22, 1993, the situation in southern Lebanon was escalating to a point of imminent war. That day, there were reports of heavy Israeli shelling of a number of villages in the south that had caused serious damage and casualties among the civilian population, and of the death of another Israeli soldier in the Israeli-occupied area.[214] The Israeli daily *Ha'aretz*, quoting unidentified military sources, reported the next day that "Israel will now wait to see whether the terrorists 'have understood the IDF's aggressive message,' as expressed by the massive artillery barrage aimed at villages north of the security zone." The same sources were then quoted as saying:

> Every katyusha fired by the terrorists toward northern settlements would constitute a crossing of the red lines. If this happens, we will have no choice other than to launch a massive operation, which could result in many casualties not only to the terrorists, but also to civilians who will not escape from their homes.[215]

This warning was clearly not heeded by Hizballah on the Lebanese side of the border, because in the early hours of Friday, July 23, several Katyushas were fired at the Galilee panhandle.[216] Although the Katyushas caused neither damage nor injuries, the response was not long in coming. Israel's "inner cabinet," a small group of the most senior government ministers, met later that Friday. Although

---

[213] "Amal claims Responsibility for Katyusha Attack," Voice of the Mountain, July 15, 1993, in FBIS-NES-93-134, July 15, 1993, p. 36.

[214] "Israelis Reportedly Withdraw Reinforcements," Radio Lebanon, July 21, 1993, and "Israeli Soldier Killed in Hizballah Attack," AFP, July 22, 1993, both in FBIS-NES-93-139, July 22, 1993, p. 21.

[215] "IDF sources Say Katyusha Firings Cross Red Line," *Ha'aretz*, July 23, 1993, in FBIS-NES-93-140, July 23, 1993, p. 15.

[216] "Katyusha Land in Galilee," Qol Yisra'el, July 23, 1993, in FBIS-NES-93-140, July 23, 1993, pp. 15-16.

there was no public announcement, evidently a decision was made then to mount a full-scale operation in Lebanon.[217]

These developments in Israel were closely monitored in Lebanon. Later that same day, Radio Free Lebanon reported that Muhammad Fadlallah, the Lebanese Shi'a community's spiritual leader, had warned that "if Israel continues to follow the policy of scorched earth and shelling civilians, the resistance will be compelled to follow the same policy with the Israelis." Fadlallah also was quoted as saying, "we will turn their land into scorched earth and kill their women, children and the elderly if they harm and shell the civilians [in Lebanon], not the mujahidin."[218]

There was one more day of quiet: Saturday, July 24, the Jewish Sabbath. The next morning, Sunday, July 25, 1993, the Israeli operation began.

Operation Accountability Unfolds

> On Sunday, July 25, at about 9:30 a.m., a war plane targeted and then destroyed my home. Three persons died in this attack: my son, Ali Kamel Balhas, nineteen; my nephew, Kamal Badi' Balhas, seventeen; and my cousin, Hala Hoballah Balhas, twenty-eight, who was nine months pregnant. My nephew Muhammad Hassan Balhas, who is nine, suffered head injuries and is still being treated at the American University Hospital [in Beirut]; doctors say he is expected to recover fully. Those who were killed and injured were sitting drinking tea in the house at the time when it was bombed. There had not been any warning. I have no idea why they targeted my house. To my knowledge,

---

[217] References to this meeting by the "inner cabinet" were made by other cabinet ministers following the start of the operation on July 25. Israel Television Network, July 25, 1993, in FBIS-NES-93-141, July 26, 1993, p. 36.

[218] "Fadlallah Vows Retaliation if Shelling Continues," Radio Free Lebanon, July 23, 1993, in FBIS-NES-93-141, July 26, 1993, p. 51. The word "mujahidin" (fighters or warriors) refers to the Hizballah guerrillas.

there was nothing of a military nature in the immediate vicinity.[219]

These are the words of a surviving relative interviewed by Human Rights Watch, describing the opening salvo of what soon became known as Operation Accountability. The air strike on the village of Seddiqin was part of the operation's first stage, which encompassed "precision" attacks by Israeli warplanes and helicopters on targets in the south, the Beqa' valley and some parts of central and northern Lebanon, as well as a shelling barrage of the outskirts of a number of villages in the south. This initial round took place between 10:30 and 11:30 in the morning, and was followed by a lull. At 2:00 p.m., the Israeli construction and housing minister Binyamin Ben-Eli'ezer declared on television that "[a]s far as we are concerned, the operation is over. The ball is now in Hizballah's court."[220]

Hizballah's response came not much later. Katyushas started landing in the Galilee in the afternoon, and by nightfall, the IDF reported that a total of fifty Katyushas had been fired, about half of which had fallen inside Israel while the other half had landed in the occupied territory.[221] That evening, a Katyusha attack on Kiryat Shemona, a town of 15,000 in northern Israel, killed two Israeli civilians

---

[219] Human Rights Watch interview with Haj Kamel Balhas, Seddiqin, October 28, 1993. Although Kamel Balhas could with justification challenge the right of the IAF under international humanitarian law to attack a civilian home in the middle of a Lebanese village, his assertion that he had "no idea" why his house was targeted is false. He was known to both Israeli intelligence and local villagers as a senior Hizballah commander. (Interviews in Seddiqin, and "Air Force Strikes Resume," IDF Radio, July 25, 1993 in FBIS-NES-93-141, July 26, 1993, p. 44). On a separate issue, it is likely that the time of the attack was 10:30 a.m. rather than 9:30 a.m. The Human Rights Watch interviews in southern Lebanon were conducted three months after the attacks; conflicting time references were very common during their interviews, and are consistent with methodological problems encountered during research of this nature in other parts of the world.

[220] "Ben-Eli'ezer Comments on Mission of Lebanon Operation," Israel Television Network, July 25, 1993, in FBIS-NES-93-131, July 26, 1993, p. 36.

[221] "Army Commanders Comment on Operation in Lebanon," IDF Radio, July 25, 1993, in FBIS-NES-93-141, July 26, 1993, p. 26.

and wounded eight others, while causing damage to dozens of apartments.[222] Several further rounds of Katyushas were to land inside Israel that evening and during the next few days, causing both damage and injuries.

Operation Accountability promptly escalated. Attacks by Israeli helicopter gunships, fighter jets and artillery were reported throughout southern Lebanon and the western Beqa' during the late afternoon and evening of Sunday, July 25, and throughout the night. By the end of the day, the IDF claimed to have hit sixty targets, "among them terrorist bases and the organization's radio station."[223] Monday morning, the shelling became more intense and was aimed at more villages. At regular intervals, the SLA started warning the population by radio to leave the area, as their Israeli allies were planning to launch a full-scale assault against Hizballah in the villages. Many people heeded these warnings and left if they had the means to do so. Others remained, either by choice or by circumstance.

In the afternoon of Monday, July 26, Israeli shells started falling inside the villages, causing massive damage and many civilian casualties. The artillery barrage continued unabated throughout the following days, tapering off only toward the end of the week. Meanwhile, the IAF continued to fly sorties and to strike at specific targets, usually particular homes inside villages or vehicles moving on the roads. Saturday, July 31, 1993, a cease-fire brokered by U.S. Secretary of State Warren Christopher came into effect at 6:00 p.m., putting an end to hostilities.

The Strategy Behind Operation Accountability

It is apparent from public statements that the operational aspects of Operation Accountability must have been planned carefully in the period leading up to July 25, and that civilians were seen as a crucial strategic element of the operation.[224] In a meeting on July 27 in which he briefed members of the Knesset

---

[222] "Two Killed in Katyusha Attack on Qiryat Shemona," Qol Yisra'el, July 25, 1993, in FBIS-NES-93-141, July 26, 1993, p. 24. These turned out to be the only Israeli fatalities during Operation Accountability.

[223] "Hizballah Targets Said Attacked," Qol Yisra'el, July 25, 1993, in FBIS-NES-93-141, July 26, 1993, p. 45.

[224] On July 26, 1993, the first day of the operation, Maj.-Gen. Me'ir Dagan, deputy head of the General Staff Operations Branch, declared: "At this stage, we cannot discuss the timeframe of the operation. It is planned in stages and with reference to developing

Foreign Affairs and Defense Committee, Prime Minister Yitzhak Rabin declared: "We want Lebanese villagers to flee and we want to damage all those who were parties to Hizballah's activities."[225]   For both these goals of Operation Accountability, Lebanese civilians were the focus.   Israel planned to drive Lebanese civilians north to Beirut in order to force the Lebanese government to crack down on Hizballah,[226] and to punish the villagers for allowing Hizballah to operate in their midst.[227]   On both counts, Israel was in grave violation of international humanitarian law which prohibits the targeting of civilians.

Driving the Population North

As highlighted by Prime Minister Rabin's statement above, one of the declared aims of Operation Accountability was to drive the inhabitants of southern Lebanese villages north in order to force the Lebanese government to rein in Hizballah.   A military action carried out with that particular aim in mind constitutes a violation of international law.   While Israel has an obligation to safeguard the security of civilians, and one legitimate way of doing so is by evacuating them from areas of military activity, denying Hizballah a social base in southern Lebanon and causing a flow of refugees as a political pressure tactic

---

situations." An Israeli reporter asked: "You talk of stages. If I understand correctly, the stages of the operation were planned before it was launched." Major General Me'ir Dagan answered, "[t]he operation is being conducted both according to the planned stages and the developing situation. Up to this moment, I can say that the situation has developed as we expected." "IDF Deputy Operations Branch Head on Lebanon," Educational Television Network, July 26, 1993, in FBIS-NES-93-141, July 26, 1993, p. 29.

[225] "Rabin Briefs Knesset Committee on Lebanese Operation," Qol Yisra'el, July 27, 1993, in FBIS-NES-93-143, July 28 1993, pp. 20-21.

[226] In the same speech quoted above, Prime Minister Yitzhak Rabin declared: "The goal of the operation is to get the southern Lebanese population to move northward, hoping that this will tell the Lebanese Government something about the refugees who may get as far north as Beirut." Ibid.

[227] On the first day of the operation, Foreign Minister Shimon Peres in an interview said of Operation Accountability: "I think it is a two-pronged effort: to strike at our attackers—that is Hizballah and other participating organizations—and to get *the attention of the pertinent populations* and governments so that they may exert pressure to end Hizballah's rampage." (Emphasis added). "Discusses Objectives of Operation," Qol Yisra'el, July 26, 1993, in FBIS-NES-93-141, July 26, 1993, p. 33.

have nothing to do with safeguarding the security of civilians. Likewise, while Israel has a right to displace civilians for imperative military reasons, such reasons also do not include political motives such as pressuring the government in Beirut.[228]

The effort to push people northward had at least three distinct stages. During the first stage, residents of southern Lebanon were warned that they were in danger and should leave their homes; during the second stage, people in villages along the front line were driven from their homes to the coastal area by intensive and prolonged shelling; and during the third stage, the displaced were driven further north along the coastal road to Beirut, seat of the Lebanese government, by the shelling of areas around the port city of Sidon.

During the first stage, Monday morning, July 26, after the air attacks on the homes of suspected Hizballah guerrilla commanders on Sunday, the IDF started shelling the environs of villages in the south, while the SLA's radio station, Voice of the South, began broadcasting messages directed at the residents of southern Lebanon, advising them to leave the area. The text of these messages varied slightly during that day and on later days, sometimes listing specific villages that were being targeted for attack. A typical message, broadcast at 2:00 p.m. Monday, was:

> We have received the following statement from responsible security sources:
>
> Following the firing of rockets on northern Israel and the border area from al-Nabatiyah last night, the Israeli army will attack Hizballah targets in the villages and towns north of the border area, including the town of al-Nabatiyah, starting at 1600 [4:00 p.m.] today.
>
> There are Hizballah elements in the town of al-Nabatiyah, including known terrorists such as Shaykh 'Adil Nadir, Samir al-Madani, and 'Abbas Rahmah alias Abu-Fadil. Their homes are bases used by the perpetrators of terrorist operations.

---

[228] While Protocol II (1977) Additional to the Geneva Conventions does not apply to the conflict between Israel and Hizballah, it does provide authoritative guidance on the humane treatment of civilians. Article 17 explicitly prohibits displacement of the civilian population for reasons related to the conflict unless the security of the civilians involved or imperative military reasons require it.

To avoid harming civilians who live in al-Nabatiyah near the terrorists' bases and houses, the security sources advise people who have not left their houses to get as far away from the area as fast as they can by 1600 today.

These sources reiterate that if calm and security do not prevail in northern Israel and the border area, neither will they prevail in al-Nabatiyah.

Our correspondent who conveyed this statement added:

As long as there are terrorists, like the three named here, among the inhabitants of al-Nabatiyah, innocent citizens will be in great danger, because Hizballah houses and offices are regarded as purely military targets.[229]

Once IDF artillery began targeting the centers of the villages on Monday afternoon, it became clear that the purpose of the radio messages was not just to warn civilians that they might be hurt if they stayed close to purported military targets, but to warn them that they would be targets if they stayed in their homes anywhere in their communities.

The warnings were especially effective once certain villages had been hit and the SLA could hold out these villages to the population of other villages as examples of what was going to happen there. This was the case with Jibshit, a village that has produced a number of senior Hizballah officials over the years and has therefore often been characterized by Israel as a hotbed of terrorism. The village was hit particularly hard during Operation Accountability. One resident there reported having heard the SLA announce on the radio: "People of Tyre and Nabatiyeh, remove the terrorists from your midst or we will do to you what we did to Jibshit."[230]

During the second stage, beginning Monday afternoon, the IDF began to target the hearts of the villages, causing civilian casualties and inducing those

---

[229] "Warning Issued to Village," Voice of the South, July 26, 1993, in FBIS-NES-93-141, July 26, 1993, p. 47.

[230] Human Rights Watch interview, Jibshit, October 24, 1993. For an example of one such announcement mentioning Jibshit, see further below.

who had braved the first wave of attacks to leave as well—as soon as they were able. Zahra Nur al-Din, a resident of Jba'a, reported:

> We didn't leave on Monday [morning] because we didn't think they were going to do what they did. However, on Monday afternoon, we were no longer able to leave because we felt it had become too dangerous [because of the shelling]. But then on Tuesday morning, it had become too dangerous to stay! We left the village at 6:30 a.m. There were very few cars, and several of them were bombed. Our own car had been damaged but was still in working order. We drove to Sidon under shellfire. We never knew if we were going to be hit or not. There were shells all the way to Kafr Malki; after that it was quiet.[231]

According to villagers, along the way to the coast Israeli planes repeatedly flew over them at low altitudes in apparent attempts to further scare people to move on. By mid-morning Tuesday, July 27, thousands of villagers were clogging the roads leading east to the coast. One eyewitness, who left his village of Majdal Silm Tuesday morning, reported that planes were firing along the sides of the roads: "I left for Beirut at 11:00 a.m., but did not arrive there until 7:00 p.m. [The journey should normally take no more than two hours]. Everyone was fleeing and there was a lot of traffic on the roads. Bombs were falling all around but none fell on the cars."[232]

The third stage of the plan to drive people north to Beirut came Tuesday, July 27. At that point villagers were flocking to the coastal towns of Tyre and Sidon and moving in with relatives there or setting up camp along the roads in the hope that the shelling would end soon. Relatively few had decided to move on to Beirut. This was soon to change. At 11:15 a.m. Tuesday, the SLA declared:

> To the people of the south: The Voice of the South transmits continuously to serve the southern citizen. Its objective is to safeguard your interest and safety. Therefore, keep listening.

---

[231] Human Rights Watch interview, Jba'a, October 25, 1993.

[232] Human Rights Watch interview, Majdal Silm, October 28, 1993.

> This is an announcement addressed to the esteemed citizens of
> Sidon and Tyre: We request the citizens of Sidon and Tyre to
> keep listening to the Voice of the South over the next few days,
> because security sources have said that the presence of facilities
> of Hizballah, the Islamic Group, and the Palestinian terrorist
> organizations near your houses will create a situation similar to
> that in Jibshit and other southern villages. Drive the terrorists
> away as soon as possible. Forewarned is forearmed.[233]

Until this time, the situation in Sidon had been relatively normal. There
had been a large influx of people from the villages, and cars continued to stream
in, but commercial life had not been interrupted by the shelling some twenty miles
away.   At the wholesale vegetable market in the Nahr Sayni area on the
southeastern outskirts of town, merchants had put in a regular business day, and
most had returned to their homes in town by mid-afternoon.   Some were still
milling around the place or drinking tea. One of them was Tal'at Ghazi, an
Egyptian migrant worker from Mansoura who said he had been in Lebanon for
only six months. At 4:00 p.m., he said, a first artillery shell landed on the
market: "I was in the shop where I work. There were maybe ten people there.
We immediately went to hide in one of the shops. Some ten shells fell on the
market between 4:00 p.m. and 1:00 a.m. Three of the guys who were there were
injured."[234] None of the workers had any idea why the market was being shelled:
there were, they said, no political, let alone military, targets in the vicinity.
    Likewise, in the Palestinian refugee camp of Ein al-Hilweh, which is
directly adjacent to the market, things had been quiet on Sunday, Monday and
most of Tuesday. The situation changed, a resident reported, in the late afternoon
of Tuesday:

> It began at 5:00 p.m. I was on the roof of our house. There
> had been shelling outside the camp [i.e., against the market,
> which is visible from the camp]. Then the shells came toward
> the camp and so we went inside the house. First, a shell landed
> 100 meters from our house. Five minutes later, a shell landed
> 200 meters away.   Then a lot of shells started coming

---

[233] "SLA Urges Citizens to Expel Hizballah," Voice of the South, July 27, 1993,
in FBIS-NES-93-142, July 27, 1993, p. 41.

[234] Human Rights Watch interview, Sidon, October 23, 1993.

down....From the first moment on, the people in the camp
began to flee to Sidon and Beirut....The shelling ended at 12:30
that night.[235]

The first shell fired at Ein al-Hilweh landed in the small backyard of a
house in the Hattin quarter of the sprawling refugee camp, where a family was
sitting in the shade of a fig tree drinking tea. Five persons were injured by
shrapnel, including a three-year-old boy, Muhammad Ahmad Shabayta.[236] As
Human Rights Watch was able to ascertain, the shells also caused severe damage
to homes.

Little more than two miles to the south of Ein al-Hilweh and the market
lies the village of Ghaziyeh, population 30,000. Ghaziyeh is a predominantly
Shi'a village, making it an exception in the Sidon area, which is generally Sunni
Muslim. That is one reason why so many people from the villages in the south
had fled to Ghaziyeh on Monday and Tuesday: many had relatives there, urban
migrants to Sidon who had settled among people of their own community. Many
of the displaced were housed in schools and empty homes. This was apparently
also the reason why Ghaziyeh was singled out among all other coastal villages for
shelling on Tuesday night: if the intent was to push the Shi'a refugees further on
to Beirut, Ghaziyeh was an ideal target. Wafa Ali Tarhini, who was born and
raised in Ghaziyeh, recounted how she became a victim:

It was Tuesday, July 27, the third day of the bombardment.
There had been no shelling of Ghaziyeh. It was nice summer
weather. People had been going about their daily business or
watching sports on TV. We were not expecting anything.
There are no military targets in Ghaziyeh. We were completely
surprised. It was eight o'clock in the evening and I was driving
through town to visit a relative. I had my sister's three children
with me in the car. Suddenly, I heard and saw shells coming
from the east. I got out of the car and ran with the children
into a house next to the road [in the center of the village]. We
ended up in a room that was filling up with people from the
neighborhood. I was standing in the doorway when a shell
exploded in an alleyway next to the house. Shrapnel came

---

[235] Human Rights Watch interview, Ein al-Hilweh, October 22, 1993.

[236] Human Rights Watch interview, Ein al-Hilweh, October 22, 1993.

flying in through the door, and I was injured in the abdomen. I was told later that my large intestine was cut. The owner of the house was also injured. I was taken to Al-Ra'i Hospital in Sidon and was immediately operated on. The first four days I remained in serious condition. I stayed a total of nine days in the hospital. I still cannot eat most things, only yoghurt and such. This is supposed to go on for another six months.[237]

Local residents report that a total of sixteen shells fell on Ghaziyeh. Five persons were injured, including one person who had just fled the shelling in Nabatiyeh. Eight houses as well as a school sustained damage in the attack. Villagers insist that they had received no advance warning.[238]

The next morning, Sidon's vegetable wholesalers returned to the market, perhaps thinking that the attack of the previous day had been an aberration. This turned out not to be the case. Khaled Aley, a Palestinian refugee originally from Safad, reported: "On Wednesday morning, the shelling resumed at 8:30. We received no warnings. We were just a little scared because of the shelling that had taken place the previous evening. But we thought it was over. This was arbitrary shelling; we did not expect it at all."[239] Tal'at Ghazi, the Egyptian quoted above, was struck by shrapnel in the leg and arm during the Wednesday morning shelling. Two persons were killed by a single shell fired at the market, Muhammad Atta, also an Egyptian migrant worker, and Fu'ad Fadel, a Lebanese merchant from Sarafand. Several other persons were injured by the same shell, including Hassaan Hassan al-Hariri whose arm had to be amputated. Some five shells exploded that morning in a span of fifteen minutes, and then quiet returned to the market. Everyone fled the area, and the market remained closed until August 3, well after the start of the cease-fire. The IDF, in a communication to Human Rights Watch, denied that any "facilities frequented largely by the general public" had been targeted.[240]

---

[237] Human Rights Watch interview, Ghaziyeh, October 21, 1993.

[238] Human Rights Watch interview with Wafa's brother, Husein Ali Tarhini, Ghaziyeh, Lebanon, October 21, 1993.

[239] Human Rights Watch interview, Sidon, October 23, 1993.

[240] Col. Ahaz Ben-Ari, head of the IDF's international law branch, in a communication to Human Rights Watch, May 18, 1994.

Following these attacks, the displaced population encamped along the roads and in schools in Sidon, as well as many people from the Sidon area, fled further north. This caused a tremendous bottleneck at the northern edge of Sidon where the coastal road narrows to two lanes as it skirts the mountainside. There is no other road to Beirut from the south, and the scene, by all accounts, was one of utter chaos.[241] Warplanes flew overhead on Tuesday and throughout the night. A hospital director in Sidon described it as follows: "They were flying at very low altitudes and breaking the sound barrier. They would do this at impossible times, like at three in the morning. This was absolutely terrifying. It is like your heart explodes; I can't really explain it to you."[242]

An estimated 300,000 civilians fled the shelling.[243] Many of these made the arduous trek along the coastal road north to Beirut. According to the director of the United Nations Relief and Works Agency (UNRWA) in Lebanon, some 50,000 Palestinian refugees left their camps. One-third of the 60,000 residents of Ein al-Hilweh moved to sites closer to Sidon. Palestinians who moved as far north as Beirut were mostly from the Tyre area; many ended up squatting along the coastal road.[244] On Wednesday, July 28, the Israeli leadership expressed "a great deal of satisfaction, far beyond what had been planned, with this exodus.

---

[241] The assertion in this regard by the Ghaziyeh witness that the shells had come from the east is significant, because it indicates that their source must have been artillery emplacements in the Jezzin salient, apparently near the village of Kafr Falus, due east from Sidon. It is from the Jezzin salient that the SLA and IDF have been able to control the main north-south artery along the coast, and it is from there that they caused and compounded the panicky scenes of tens of thousands of civilians fleeing up a two-lane road in July 1993. There was also traffic coming south from Beirut, mostly family members of villagers who were driving down hoping to evacuate their relatives from the South.

[242] Human Rights Watch interview, Sidon, October 22, 1993. Qol Yisra'el reported on Tuesday morning that "Israel Air Force aircraft are flying low over wide areas of Lebanon and are breaking the sound barrier, causing damage to property and shocking residents." "More Rockets Hit 27 Jul" [sic], in FBIS-NES-93-142, July 27, 1993, p. 22.

[243] Rathmell, "The War in South Lebanon," p. 180.

[244] Human Rights Watch interview, Beirut, October 20, 1993. The UNRWA director, Frank de Jonge, said that many of the displaced had to be housed in UNRWA schools, and that this had led to much damage. He estimated the total cost to UNRWA of sheltering the Palestinians to be $100,000.

Israel had estimated that some 100,000 people would flee, but according to current estimates 150,000 to 200,000 people have fled north."[245]

Civilian Casualties

There is no doubt that civilians in southern Lebanon bore the brunt of Operation Accountability. The Lebanese authorities, local aid agencies, and international nongovernmental organizations all agreed that the vast majority of the casualties were civilians, not guerrillas affiliated with Hizballah or some of the militant Palestinian factions.[246] Officials at local hospitals in the south, which were the first to receive casualties, are unanimous in asserting that all the dead and injured who were brought to their facilities were civilians. A sample of hospital admissions that week showed:

- Hammoud Hospital, Sidon: eighty-seven casualties (one of whom died), all civilians. In addition, thirteen were dead on arrival at the hospital.[247]
- Al-Ra'i Hospital, Sidon: forty-three casualties, all of them civilians.[248]

---

[245] IDF Radio reporting on the discussions held at a special cabinet meeting in Jerusalem on July 28, 1993. "Cabinet Session Ends; No Decisions on Operation," IDF Radio, in FBIS-NES-93-143, July 28, 1993, p. 23. The reporter added: "In any event, the prime minister and other security sources expressed a great deal of satisfaction with the pace of the exodus." By the end of October 1993, some 32,000 to 40,000 civilians, Lebanese citizens as well as Palestinian refugees, still remained displaced. Human Rights Watch interview with the head of an international relief organization. Beirut, October 19, 1993.

[246] Hizballah later claimed that seventeen of its fighters were killed during the week of July 25, both during guerrilla actions against IDF/SLA targets in the occupied border zone and in the shelling of villages by the IDF's artillery. (Human Rights Watch interview with Hassan Hoballah, head of Hizballah's international relations section, Beirut, October 20, 1993). Col. Ahaz Ben-Ari, head of the IDF's international law branch, in a communication to Human Rights Watch, May 18, 1994, stated that the IDF estimated that between fifty and eighty guerillas had been killed as a result of the military action.

[247] Human Rights Watch interview with the hospital's director, Salim Mamlouk, Sidon, October 21, 1993.

[248] Human Rights Watch interview with the hospital's director, Dr. Adel al-Ra'i, Sidon, October 21, 1993.

- Labib Abu Zahr Hospital, Sidon: thirty-six casualties, all of them civilians.[249]
- Hikmat al-Amin Hospital, Habboush: sixty-six casualties, all of them civilians.[250]
- Jabl Amal Hospital, Tyre: 234 casualties (one of whom died), all civilians except one Lebanese Army soldier who had been traveling in a civilian car at night when his car was attacked by a helicopter. In addition, twenty-four persons were dead on arrival at the hospital.[251]

The high incidence of children and older men and women on casualty lists obtained from the above and other hospitals supports the hospital officials' claim that most if not all of the patients were civilians. At the Jabl Amal Hospital in Tyre, for example, one-third of the 234 injured persons brought to the hospital that week were children under nineteen, and another one-fifth were persons age fifty and over.[252] There is no evidence to suggest that any of the adults brought to that hospital were combatants. Military casualties, one hospital official asserted, were sent directly to Rasoul al-Azm Hospital in Beirut; another said that Hizballah had suffered very few casualties because "the military people were able to hide."[253]

International law enjoins belligerents to refrain from indiscriminate fire and to adhere to the principle of proportionality when selecting targets to attack. The IDF took great pains to deny that any indiscriminate bombardment had taken place at any time during Operation Accountability. The specific targets of the

---

[249] Human Rights Watch interview with the hospital's administrative director, Mouin Abu Zahr, Sidon, October 22, 1993.

[250] Human Rights Watch interview with Dr. Ahmad Mushawrab, program director and general surgeon at the hospital, Habboush, October 22, 1993.

[251] Human Rights Watch interview with Dr. Ahmad al-Mruweh, a surgeon at the hospital, Tyre, October 27, 1993.

[252] Admissions list for casualties of Operation Accountability for Jabl Amal Hospital in Tyre, provided to Human Rights Watch by the hospital administration, October 1993. The precise figures are: Children 0-18 years old: 32.5 percent; adults aged 19-49: 42.7 percent; adults aged 50 and over: 21.8 percent; persons age unknown: 2.1 percent. (Figures do not add up to 100 percent due to rounding).

[253] Human Rights Watch interviews, October 1993.

operation, it said, were weapon caches, guerrilla headquarters and training camps. Any damage which occurred to hospitals, dispensaries, schools, places of worship, cemeteries, ambulances and electrical and water supply systems was merely incidental and "entirely in proportion with the concrete and direct military advantage gained from the Operation."[254] The casualty toll and extensive damage inflicted on civilian population centers belie this claim.

The IDF. has tried to justify the number of civilian casualties and the high rate of damage to civilian property by accusing Hizballah of shielding military targets with civilians. Israel's chief of general staff, Lt.-Gen. Ehud Barak, said on July 26: "We believe that those elements who...fire at us from within civilian settlements are responsible for the civilian casualties [and] Hizballah is responsible for the suffering caused to the civilian population which is being driven out of its homes because it continues firing at us from inside and from the outskirts of Lebanese villages."[255] Timor Goksel, the UNIFIL spokesman in Lebanon, claimed in October 1993 that, in his experience, Hizballah has not fired Katyushas from inside villages.[256] Human Rights Watch is not in a position to say whether Hizballah has fired from within civilian population centers, although we are aware of several cases, including one in the village of al-Qleileh described below, in which Hizballah appears to have fired from within the vicinity of civilian population centers. In doing so, Hizballah may be in violation of the injunction (Protocol I, Art. 58(b)) to avoid locating military objectives within or near densely populated areas or the injunction (Protocol I, Art. 51(7)) against using civilians as a shield for military objectives or operations. (See also chapter 3 above).

However, as the party that was shelling and bombarding these civilian areas, the IDF is obliged not merely to assert but to provide proof that Hizballah

---

[254] Col. Ahaz Ben-Ari of the international law division of the IDF, in a communication to Human Rights Watch, May 18, 1994.

[255] "Baraq: Hizballah Responsible for Action," Qol Yisra'el, July 26, 1993, in FBIS-NES-93-141, July 26, 1993, p. 28.

[256] Human Rights Watch interview, Tyre, October 27, 1993. There are some reports, however, that Hizballah may have used UNIFIL positions as cover. Robert Fisk, for example, reported one incident during Operation Accountability when "[Hezbollah] even hauled a Russian-made Katyusha launcher up to the very rear of the Irish UN battalion's Position 6-42 east of Haris and fired off three missiles toward the Israelis." *The Independent*, July 30, 1995.

guerrillas and other combatants in southern Lebanon have in fact used villages as shields for military activities—just as it is obliged to show that the civilian damage inflicted in southern Lebanon was proportionate to the military advantage gained. Above and beyond that, even if the IDF can establish that guerrillas are operating from within population centers, it must still seek to minimize any civilian casualties resulting from its legitimate targeting of military objects. Human Rights Watch is concerned that IDF forces directed fire toward villages located closest to the source of Katyusha attacks during Operation Accountability without identifying or targeting specific military objectives there,[257] without regard for possible civilian casualties, and possibly even as reprisal for military actions by guerrillas forces.

This seemed to be the case with an attack that took place in the village of al-Qleileh in the Tyre area on Wednesday, July 28. On the previous three days, the village had been shelled only sporadically.[258] But that morning, according to a witness interviewed by Human Rights Watch, there was some IDF/SLA shelling near the entrance of the village, and shortly after 8:30 he saw a Katyusha being fired by Lebanese guerrillas from fields outside the village. The witness, Hassan Darwish, had spent the night with some seventy members of his extended family in the basement of his employer's house on the edge of the village;[259] his boss had left the village with his family for Tyre the previous Sunday to escape the shelling. By 8:30 that morning, a number of persons had left the makeshift shelter to get food and take care of other essential business; forty-two remained inside. Mr. Darwish had also temporarily left the shelter to get food for his family from his own house, and when he saw the Katyusha being launched, he rushed back to the shelter, expecting an Israeli response. In his words:

---

[257] Protocol I expressly prohibits indiscriminate attacks, which it defines, in Article 51(4)(a), as attacks "which are not directed at a specific military objective."

[258] The admissions list of Jabl Amal Hospital in Tyre for casualties during Operation Accountability shows no admissions from al-Qleileh for July 25 or 26, and seven casualties from that village on Tuesday, July 27, including three children and one old man. Human Rights Watch has no information about the cause of the injuries on July 27, but witnesses reported shelling on the village that day.

[259] The witness referred to the basement as a shelter, but most basements in southern Lebanon seen by Human Rights Watch appeared better protected that the basement in this particular house. It is located underneath a terrace attached to the house facing the front line, and is therefore exposed from both the side and above.

Shortly after I returned to the shelter, my wife, who had been at the door on her way out to get a hose, came back in to tell me that she had seen a helicopter. The moment she said that, a rocket struck the shelter, coming through the ceiling. One of my cousins, a boy of fourteen, Husein Mustafa Darwish, was killed. His sister, Fatma Mustafa Darwish, suffered facial burns, and Sekna Mahmoud Amer lost an eye in that attack.[260]

We all tried to leave the shelter. When I came out, I saw the helicopter hovering in the air. It fired a second rocket at us, which also slammed through the ceiling. People were hurt by splinters from the tiles that broke off the terrace above the basement. There were many facial injuries then, especially among the children.

The helicopter fired a third rocket, this time at the door of the shelter, but it didn't explode. We were all trying to get away from the house, while the injured people stayed near the shelter. We wanted to get them into cars and take them to hospital in Tyre. A fourth rocket was fired but landed far from us. Once we had managed to remove the wounded persons, I went back to get the dead boy. His' parents were with him. When I came out of the shelter with the boy and his parents, the helicopter fired two more rockets at us. The first of these didn't do any harm, but the second hurt the parents. The boy's mother lost part of her foot. Then an ambulance came and took the mother and the boy. The father was taken away in a pick-up truck. The helicopter fired bullets at the ambulance, but didn't hit it. It also fired one more rocket, but that one didn't hurt anyone.

---

[260] When Human Rights Watch inspected the site in October 1993, the two entry holes in the ceiling (floor of the terrace) had visibly been repaired. Numerous pieces of dried human flesh remained stuck against the ceiling.

According to Mr. Darwish, some twenty-two persons sustained injuries requiring their hospitalization as a result of the attack.[261]

The IDF appears to have targeted a broad spectrum of civilians as if they were combatants in the conflict, identifying political members or even sympathizers of Hizballah and relatives as among those who could legitimately be targeted, and even shelling entire villages. Setting the framework, Israel's chief of general staff, Lt.-Gen. Ehud Barak, declared: "We regard Hizballah, the population which harbors it, and the Lebanese regime which permits all this activity as responsible."[262] A comment from an Israeli gunner perhaps best summed up this approach: "[M]ost of the civilians are Hezbollah."[263] International humanitarian law expressly forbids indiscriminate attacks. Article 51(4)(a) of Protocol I defines indiscriminate attacks as "those which are not directed at a specific military objective," and Article 51(5)(a) includes among indiscriminate attacks "an attack by bombardment by any methods or means which treats as a single military objective a number of clearly separated and distinct military objectives located in a city, town, village or other area containing a similar concentration of civilians or civilian objects." (See also the section on physical damage below).[264]

---

[261] Human Rights Watch interview, al-Qleileh, October 27, 1993. The admissions list of the Jabl Amal Hospital in Tyre shows that twenty-six persons from al-Qleileh were admitted to the hospital on July 28. Of these, sixteen were children, eight were women, and two were men over age fifty. Human Rights Watch has no information whether or not the ambulance that was attacked by the helicopter was clearly marked.

[262] "Rabin, Baraq Comment on Operation's Objectives," Israel Television Network, July 26, 1993 in FBIS-NES-93-142, July 27, 1993, p. 24. Barak presently serves as foreign minister in the government of Prime Minister Shimon Peres.

[263] Julian Ozanne and Mark Nicholson, "Israel steps up artillery attacks on south Lebanon," *Financial Times*, July 28, 1993.

[264] The ICRC commentary clarifies this provision further: "In fact, areas of land between military objectives are not themselves military objectives. It must be accepted that in open areas which are sparsely populated, such as forests, attacks may be mounted against the whole of the area if it has been established that enemy armed forces are present. On the other hand, in a town, village or any other area where there is a similar concentration of civilian persons and objects, the military objectives in that area may only be attacked separately without leading to civilian losses outside the military objectives themselves. This also applies for temporary concentrations of civilians, such as refugee camps." International

The IDF's blatant disregard for the letter and spirit of international humanitarian law was paired with an apparent inability, or unwillingness, to assess in a meaningful way the extent of the casualties inflicted on the civilian population in southern Lebanon. Indeed, while Brig.-Gen. Amir Dror of the Intelligence Branch was able to report that about twenty Hizballah members were killed and twenty wounded,[265] Maj.-Gen. Herzl Budinger, commander of the Air Force could only conclude that, "[u]nfortunately, we also hit civilians, but fortunately very few."[266]

Senior commanders were candid in stating that the homes of Hizballah members were seen as legitimate targets of attack. The head of the IDF's Intelligence Branch, Maj.-Gen. Uri Sagi, declared on the first day of the assault, July 25, that "today, the 16 targets selected and attacked were mostly bases, offices, or living quarters of Hizballah operatives."[267] Broadcast warnings also made it clear that Hizballah homes were considered legitimate military targets.[268] Human Rights Watch is in no position to determine whether the "Hizballah operatives" referred to were civilian or military officials. If they were civilians, then targeting of their homes would have been a direct violation of the injunction against attacks on civilians. If, however, some of these officials were military commanders, Human Rights Watch is concerned whether adequate warning was given to the civilians resident in those homes allegedly used as "bases," and whether the risk of civilian casualties was excessive in proportion to the concrete and direct military advantage anticipated. The burden is on the IDF to supply specific information about its targets so as to substantiate the assertion that the "living quarters of Hizballah operatives" constituted legitimate military targets.

Committee of the Red Cross, *Commentary on the Additional Protocols* (Geneva: Martinus Nijhoff Publishers, 1987), p. 624 (par. 1973).

[265] "IDF Officers Review Lebanon Operation 27 Jul" [sic], Qol Yisra'el, July 27, 1993, in FBIS-NES-93-143, July 28, 1993, p. 17.

[266] Ibid.

[267] "Army Commanders Comment on Operation in Lebanon," IDF Radio, July 25, 1993, in FBIS-NES-93-141, July 26, 1993, p. 27. Lt.-Gen. Ehud Barak, chief of general staff, declared in the same radio program: "[W]e singled out another 40 homes, mainly those of key Hizballah operatives throughout the strip of villages along the northern part of the security zone." Ibid., p. 26.

[268] See the excerpt from an SLA radio broadcast above.

One example of the targeting of the house of a suspected Hizballah operative is provided by the testimony of Husein Ali Hayek. According to Mr. Hayek, one of his relatives was a member of Hizballah who used to visit their house in Kafr Tibnit from time to time, but he was not present in the village during Operation Accountability. On Monday, July 26, according to Mr. Hayek:

> The shelling [of the area around the village] began in the morning and continued all day. No one was injured in this. That day, the SLA announced on the radio that anyone living near Hizballah should leave. We didn't actually hear this on the radio, but people told us about it. We decided to stay because we do not belong to any of the parties. We thought we had nothing to fear.

At 10:30 the next morning, July 27, as Mr. Hayek and twenty-two members of his extended family, all of them civilians who occupy a cluster of four homes in the village, were huddling in the basement of Mr. Hayek's house because of the heavy shelling, they heard the sound of three airplanes. Mr. Hayek recalled what happened next:

> We were inside the house. We heard a huge explosion and then the house came down on us. We couldn't breathe because of the dust. The whole family was in the house, including my father, a total of twenty-three persons. My brother Majed died instantly from shrapnel that struck him in the head. My brother Fu'ad was injured by shrapnel and glass all over his body, and he still has a piece of glass stuck inside his thigh. My brother Fawzi was struck by shrapnel vertically across his chest and throat, and he still is unable to use his voice. We know from the craters that there must have been a total of nine bombs.

When asked what the possible motive for the targeting of the house might have been, Mr. Hayek said:

> It is possible that they bombed our four homes because my cousin is with Hizballah. He was living in my uncle's home, which was also destroyed, but the people were all in my house at the time of the attack. My cousin who is with Hizballah was not here at the time. My brother Majed, who was killed, had

been living in Germany, where he had obtained asylum. He had planned to return to Germany the next day.[269]

Another air attack on the home of a senior Hizballah leader in Lebanon, Kamel Balhas, in the village of Seddiqin on July 25, resulted in three deaths: a pregnant woman, a nephew and a son of Kamel Balhas, while a nine-year-old boy sustained head injuries.[270]

During Operation Accountability, the IDF also executed what appear to have been calculated direct attacks on purely civilian targets. One such series of attacks was carried out against Sidon's wholesale vegetable market on Tuesday, July 27 and Wednesday, July 28. These attacks, described in more detail above, were executed without warning, and were probably intended both to terrify local residents into leaving their homes and to push further northwards refugees who had sought safety in the Sidon area. At least two people were killed and six injured in the attacks on the market. The market itself was frequented by the public and the area had no apparent military or even political targets. The same intent—to instill fear among civilians—appears to have prompted the attack on the adjacent Palestinian refugee camp of Ein al-Hilweh on July 27.

Ineffective Warnings

Article 57(2)(c) of Protocol I to the Geneva Conventions demands that effective advance warning be given of attacks that may affect the civilian population, unless circumstances do not allow.[271] If civilians do not or cannot heed these warnings, the attacker is not relieved from the obligation to avoid indiscriminate attacks under Article 51, and the principle of proportionality

---

[269] Human Rights Watch interview, Kafr Tibnit, October 23, 1993. Husein's father and his two injured brothers Fu'ad and Fawzi, as well as other relatives who had been in the house at the time of the attack, were present at the time of the interview.

[270] The case is described in more detail toward the beginning of this chapter. See also, "Air Force Strikes Resume," IDF Radio, July 25, 1993, in FBIS-NES-93-141, July 26, 1993, p. 44.

[271] Article 57 (2) (c) of Protocol I states: "effective advance warning shall be given of attacks which may affect the civilian population, unless circumstances do not permit."

continues to apply.[272] The relevant questions to ask in the context of Operation Accountability are whether the IDF/SLA could or should have known that civilians would not heed the warnings; whether they could or should have known that civilians could not flee; and whether the attacks that followed the warnings could be described as attacks aimed at civilian objects or area bombardment, or in some other way plainly outside the calculus of proportionality. In the view of Human Rights Watch, the content of the warnings, especially those issued during the early stages of the operation, was such as to confuse civilians about the nature of the targets selected for attack. It was therefore reasonably foreseeable that a segment of the population might not flee, and it was entirely foreseeable that in particular the old and indigent would not be able to evacuate their homes, especially considering the brevity of time between the first warnings and the beginning of the shelling. The attacks that followed—the wholesale shelling of civilian areas—clearly violated the principle of proportionality.

Moreover, as the stated objective of the Israeli government was to foment a refugee flow in order to put pressure on the Lebanese government to rein in Hizballah, the intention of the warnings and subsequent shelling may well have been to sow terror among the civilian population. As emphasized above, the

---

[272] Even attacks on legitimate military targets are limited by the principle of proportionality. This principle places a duty on the attacker to choose means of attack that avoid or minimize damage to civilians, and to refrain from launching an attack if the expected civilian casualties would outweigh the importance of the military target to the attacker. The principle is codified in Protocol I, Article 51(5):

> Among others, the following types of attacks are to be considered as indiscriminate:...

> (b) an attack which may be expected to cause incidental loss of civilian life, injury to civilians, damage to civilian objects, or a combination thereof, which would be excessive in relation to the concrete and direct military advantage anticipated.

If an attack can be expected to cause incidental civilian casualties or damage, two requirements must be met before that attack is launched. First, there must be an anticipated "concrete and direct military advantage." To be "concrete and direct," such an advantage must not be vague or to be gained at some unknown time in the future, such as establishing conditions conducive to an eventual surrender; it must consist of ground gained or a tangible weakening of the enemy armed forces. The second requirement is that the foreseeable civilian casualties or damage not be disproportionate, that is "excessive" in comparison to the expected "concrete and direct" military advantage.

targeting of whole villages without distinction of specific military objectives constitutes a violation of Article 51(4) and (5) of Protocol I. Additionally, the issuing of warnings with the intent to cause terror constitutes a violation of Article 51(2), which states, in part: "Acts or threats of violence the primary purpose of which is to spread terror among the civilian population are prohibited." While Israel has claimed that warnings to the civilian population were made with a view to protecting civilians from collateral injury in attacks on strictly military objectives, a number of factors make it reasonable to assume that the intention was in fact to sow terror among the civilian population. As the pattern of physical damage showed (see further below), the IDF/SLA subjected entire villages to area bombardment. In addition, the SLA radio station broadcast threats of a general nature, warning anyone remaining in certain areas that they would be in danger of being hit. The threats and the nature of the attacks combined make clear that in significant areas in southern Lebanon whole populations—indeed anyone who failed to flee by a certain time—were targeted as if they were combatants.[273]

Civilians in southern Lebanon were either attacked by surprise—before any warnings were issued—or they were not in a position to respond to warnings broadcast by the SLA that the population should flee and were pinned down in their homes by the intense shell fire that followed. Consider the case of the Balhas family in Seddiqin, referred to above, whose home was struck by the IAF during the first wave of attacks Sunday morning, July 25, 1993. The family was sitting inside drinking tea—this was before the first warnings of Operation Accountability had been broadcast. In a similar attack, seven civilians were reported killed in the village of Janta in the Beqa' valley Sunday. In the village of Zabqin, six persons (including four children and one 75-year-old woman) were injured in a helicopter attack on four homes on Sunday; some of their relatives were said to belong to Hizballah, but these persons were reportedly not home at

---

[273] Article 33 of the Fourth Geneva Convention also states, in part: "Collective penalties and likewise all measures of intimidation or of terrorism are prohibited." The ICRC Commentary provides the rationale for this prohibition: "During past conflicts, the infliction of collective penalties has been intended to forestall breaches of the law rather than to repress them; in resorting to intimidatory measures to terrorise the population, the belligerents hoped to prevent hostile acts. Far from achieving the desired effect, however, such practices, by reason of their excessive severity and cruelty, kept alive and strengthened the spirit of resistance. They strike at guilty and innocent alike. They are opposed to all principles based on humanity and justice and it is for that reason that the prohibition of collective penalties is followed formally by the prohibition of all measures of intimidation or terrorism with regard to protected persons, wherever they may be." Pictet, pp. 225-26.

the time of the attack. In the same village, according to villagers, IDF/SLA artillery began targeting the homes around three o'clock that afternoon, more than twelve hours before the first radio warnings were issued.[274]

Once the SLA started broadcasting its warnings to the population on Monday, July 26, the nature of the warnings was either so general or so misleading that many people apparently did not to take them seriously. In one warning, the SLA's Voice of the South declared at 2:00 p.m. that day: "[T]he Israeli Army will attack Hizballah targets in the villages and towns north of the border area, including the town of al-Nabatiyah, starting at 16:00 today."[275] One person interviewed by Human Rights Watch, Leila Hassan Aloush, a Palestinian refugee living in Kafr Ruman, close to Nabatiyeh, explained:

> On Monday, at 11:00 or 12:00, there were warnings on their [SLA] radios that people living near Hizballah houses should leave. So we stayed. We had nothing to fear. There are no Hizballah houses in the neighborhood. There are only civilians living here, no military.

Leila Aloush and her cousin Munifa Ali Saleh were grievously injured by an artillery shell while inside Ms. Saleh's house at around 3:30 or 4 o'clock later that afternoon.[276]

In some villages further removed from the frontline, residents who had fled after the first air raids on Sunday, July 25, started returning Tuesday when they saw that their village was not being shelled and heard no specific threats in SLA broadcasts. They became targets when the IDF expanded its campaign. This happened, for example, in Kafr Malki, on the road from Sidon to villages in the Iqlim al-Tuffah. One eyewitness reported:

---

[274] Human Rights Watch interview, Zabqin, October 27, 1993. The six persons injured in the attack were Nazar Bzey'a (female, 75), Ali Meslim (male, 12), Masar Bzey'a (female, 4), As'ad Bzey'a (male, 22), Suzanne Bzey'a (female, 6), and Sajida Bzey'a (female, 3).

[275] "Warnings Issued to Village," Voice of the South, in FBIS-NES-93-141, July 26, 1993, p. 47.

[276] Human Rights Watch interview, Kafr Ruman, October 22, 1993. For a more detailed description of this incident, see the section on the use of phosphorus below.

It began at 9:45 in the morning on Wednesday, July 28. Planes swooped down and began bombing houses in the village. One man was killed in the first raid, Mahmoud Ghassein, twenty-two, an engineering student in Russia who had come home for his vacation, and twelve people were injured. After ten minutes, there was a second raid. A house that was struck collapsed on two women, Zanoub al-Mir, fifty, and Fatmeh Qasem, who was eighty. At noon, planes flew over without bombing the village; they broke the sound barrier repeatedly, making an awful noise. Then, between 2:30 and 4:00 in the afternoon, the Arabic service of Israel Radio announced that "the IDF warns the people of Kafr Malki and Humin al-Fowqa to leave their villages." This was too late![277]

Some people said that they had failed to take the warnings seriously because on previous occasions when threats had been made, nothing of consequence had occurred. Villages in the area had been shelled repeatedly for years, and residents had learned to cope with this. In Kafr Ruman, for example, a village on the front line directly underneath the guns of the IDF and SLA, an eyewitness told Human Rights Watch that villagers had heard the SLA's warnings in time. But, he said, "we had experienced these warnings before. About a year earlier, in fact, the Israelis used loudspeakers to warn us to leave, but then they ended up shelling us only a little bit. We thought this time that it was a bit of a joke, really. Who could imagine that they would be serious about displacing a whole town?"[278]

The broadcasting of warnings in no way entitled the IDF to assume that villages would be empty of a civilian population[279] and in no way justified the

---

[277] Human Rights Watch interview, Kafr Malki, October 25, 1993. According to the same witness, the IDF also started lobbing artillery rounds at Kafr Malki that same morning of Wednesday, July 28, 1993.

[278] Human Rights Watch interview, Kafr Ruman, October 31, 1993.

[279] Maj.-Gen. Amnon Shahak, Israel's deputy chief of staff, declared on July 28, "there has been a massive flight of the population from the entire south....we estimate that most of the villages in the South have become almost totally empty." "IDF Officers Review Lebanon Operation 27 Jul" [sic], Qol Yisra'el, July 27, 1993, in FBIS-NES-93-143, July 28, 1993, p. 17.

conclusion of Brig.-Gen. Amir Dror of the IDF's intelligence branch who asserted that "as the civilian population leaves, a higher percentage of the people in the area are Hizballa [sic] terrorists as well as a few terrorists from the Palestinian organizations."[280] Unfortunately, as Human Rights Watch found, it was actually the weakest members of the population, the elderly and the poor, who were unable to flee their villages, who became the principal victims of the shelling.

It is clear from witness accounts that the vast majority of the Lebanese population started taking the threats seriously only once the IDF began to shell villages on Monday, July 26, 1993. It is also apparent from interviews that many young men, regardless of their political affiliation, stayed behind because they thought that the IDF might launch a ground offensive and they wanted to be prepared to defend their villages. But the majority of those who stayed were older folks who either had limited mobility, felt that they had to take care of their livestock, or simply did not want to leave. A resident in his sixties from Kafra, on the border of the Israeli-occupied area, said:

> On Monday, at 7:00 a.m., we heard warnings on the SLA radio that all people in the villages in this area should leave before 10:00 and that after that, people would stay at their own risk. The shelling began at 11:00, but even before that planes had been scaring people who were walking along the roads; these were people who were fleeing the village. Many people in the village don't have cars. The warning was repeated on the radio every hour. I stayed because I did not want to leave and because I felt it was safer to hide here. I stayed in my home for seven days. All the old people in the village, maybe a hundred, stayed behind. I never left my house except to feed the cattle and check up on the neighbors who are elderly relatives of mine. It was dangerous to move about.[281]

Those who stayed behind have described their experience as terrifying. Deprived of electricity (which was cut during the early stages of the attack), often also of drinking water, and unable to communicate with the outside world, they

---

[280] Ibid.

[281] Human Rights Watch interview, Kafra, October 28, 1993.

stayed huddled in the basements of their homes for days, living on bread and other food that had happened to be in the house when the fighting first broke out.

Others had no transportation, or no place to go to and no money to pay for a hotel in Tyre, Sidon or Beirut. A man in Jba'a said he and his family had been unable to leave "because we had no car, and drivers were charging between 40,000 and 50,000 pounds [U.S.$23 to $29, a great deal of money for the region] per person. And then, where could we have gone? Sleep out in the street?" So he stayed behind with his wife, six children, a sister, and elderly mother when most other people fled as shells rained down around the village on Monday. They moved to another house in Jba'a because their own house was freestanding and therefore more exposed. Then, he recalled:

> On Tuesday, there was heavy shelling, and all the houses in the village were affected. We remained forty-eight hours without food or water. This was on Tuesday and Wednesday. Until that time, there had been no bombing from the air.

> On Wednesday, I don't really know what happened, because we were staying in the basement of a house in our neighborhood, but it seems that the planes started their strikes that day. That evening, we were able to move to a house that we thought was safer because it had two floors below ground level. But later that evening, a shell struck the house, destroying the three top floors. We thought we were going to die right there and then. We were able to see the moon, because the ceiling had suddenly gone. But when we saw the moon, at least we knew we were still alive!

> We called out the names of all the persons who had been with us, and whoever answered we knew was all right. Only one twenty-five-year-old man did not answer, and we thought that he had died, so we left him for the moment. But after about half an hour he came to, and it turned out that he had suffered only a slight injury.

> So then we returned to the house where we had been staying earlier that day. The attacks continued. Inside, we didn't know what was happening outside. It was impossible to get any sleep, and we had no food or water. Nobody was able to come

and help us; nobody was able to reach the village from outside. Many animals died, both from the shelling and from lack of food. We stayed in hiding until Saturday afternoon. The damage was complete. Every hour I felt as if I was growing a thousand years older.[282]

People who were injured remained without help. Some people died of natural causes during that week; their relatives were unable to bury them until after the cease-fire late Saturday, July 31. None of the villages in southern Lebanon visited by Human Rights Watch had air raid shelters; residents tended to move to houses that had the most secure basements.

The villagers became victims of the IDF's dual strategy. If they fled, they became victims of the IDF's scheme, in the words of the Israeli prime minister, Yitzhak Rabin, to "put pressure on the Beirut government and hit those who collaborate with Hezbollah."[283] But if they stayed in their homes, they fell victim to the other component of the campaign, the aim of which was, according to Gen. Yehosh Dorfman, commander of the artillery corps, "to destroy the villages and the houses of the activists and the locations from which the rockets are fired."[284]

Blocking Access to Medical Care and Emergency Relief

During Operation Accountability the IDF at times hindered and even attacked ambulances and vehicles of relief organizations, and carried out a number of attacks on persons attempting to flee the area. At 10:00 p.m. on Tuesday, July 27, the SLA made the following announcement on the radio:

> Citing a reliable source, our correspondent reports the following:
>
> In order to stop the firing of artillery [sic] shells toward Israel and the security area, the Israeli Army has decided to hit all

---

[282] Human Rights Watch interview, Jba'a, October 25, 1993.

[283] "More Israeli Attacks Reported in South 28 Jul" [sic], AFP, July 28, 1993, in FBIS-NES-93-143, July 28, 1993, p. 36.

[284] Chris Hedges, "Israel Keeps Pounding South Lebanon," *New York Times*, July 29, 1993.

means of transportation moving on civilian and military roads in three areas that we will specify later. The word area is meant to include the village or the township itself, the roads leading to them or around them, and the open lands that surround the village houses. Here are the details of the three areas:

The first area is that of Jibshit.

The second area includes the following villages and townships: [eight villages in the Nabatiyeh area named].

The third area includes the following villages and townships: [eleven villages in the Tibnin area named].

All means of transportation seen moving during the night, starting from the time this statement is transmitted, will be regarded as a purely military target and will be hit by the Israeli Army's fire.

Anyone who does not heed these instructions for his own safety will subject himself to danger at his own risk.[285]

The warnings effectively turned whole areas of southern Lebanon into free-fire zones, in direct violation of the prohibition in Protocol I, cited above, on indiscriminate attacks. A resident of Jibshit said that he had heard the SLA announce a similar threat as early as two o'clock on Tuesday afternoon, specifying that the ban on traffic would start at 7:00 p.m.[286] In reality, the first casualties came earlier. At 5:00 p.m., in full daylight, three men reportedly died when their car was struck by a rocket fired by a helicopter on the road from Jibshit to nearby Abbeh in the direction of the coast. At 7:30 p.m., four persons were injured when their car was hit on the road from Jibshit to Ansar (also leading to the coast). The next day, three more men were killed while driving

---

[285] "Israelis Warn Against Road Traffic," Voice of the South, 10:09 p.m., July 27, 1993, in FBIS-NES-93-143, July 28, 1993, p. 35. Note the radio's mention of "a reliable source," a probable reference to the SLA's Israeli partners.

[286] Human Rights Watch interview, Jibshit, October 24, 1993.

their car near Dweir, while on Wednesday evening, a man called Yusef al-Diyab was killed near Jibshit.[287] An off-duty Lebanese Army soldier driving in a civilian car was killed at night in the Tyre area, and two other persons were struck by helicopter rockets in broad daylight: a person from Dirdghaya, at 10:00 a.m., and a man from Sha'biya, at 6:00 p.m.[288] At 6:45 p.m. on Wednesday, a car carrying two passengers on the road between Tibnin and Sultaniya was attacked by a fighter jet; both were killed.[289] Several more civilians are reported to have been injured or killed in their cars as a result of air strikes on Tuesday and the days that followed.

U.N. cars and Red Cross ambulances were not exempt from attack. One U.N. official told Human Rights Watch:

> The Israelis issued warnings via the radio and TV that they were going to shell certain areas from such and such a time, and they advised people that they should leave within a certain time period. This started on July 25 and was very effective. They also banned all traffic, saying they would regard it as hostile, including U.N. vehicles. They said they couldn't distinguish civilian from U.N. vehicles. This is bullshit.[290]

At least three, possibly four or five, ambulances were hit during that week. In the first incident, on Sunday, July 25, an ambulance of the Lebanese

---

[287] Human Rights Watch interview, Jibshit, October 24, 1993. The names of the men reported killed near Abbeh are: Muhammad Khalil Fahhas, Muhammad Hammoud and Qasem Shayteneh; the names of the Dweir casualties are: Jamal Jouni, Hassan Rammal and Husein Ramadan.

[288] Human Rights Watch interview with a surgeon at Jabl Amal Hospital, Tyre, October 27, 1993. It is not clear on which days these three attacks took place, but regardless of whether warnings had been issued, and short of evidence presented by the IDF that these vehicles constituted legitimate military objects, there was no justification for firing at civilian vehicles.

[289] Human Rights Watch interview, Tibnin, October 28, 1993. The name of one of the victims is Khader Wahhab; the identity of the second man remains unclear, but it may have been Nimri Ajami, a man in his sixties who, like Khader Wahhab, was from Majdal Silm.

[290] Human Rights Watch interview, Beirut, October 20, 1993.

Red Cross was struck by shrapnel near Da'meh when a rocket fired by a helicopter hit a nearby building in the aftermath of the IAF's attack on the base of the PFLP-GC in that area. A few days later, an ambulance of the Lebanese Red Cross traveling between Tibnin and Sultaniyeh was hit by shrapnel from shells at three o'clock in the afternoon. No one was hurt. Both ambulances had clear Red Cross markings.[291] A third ambulance was reported fired at by a helicopter in Kafra; this incident could not be independently confirmed, but the same helicopter reportedly also fired at the Red Cross clinic in the village. The clinic, which bore Red Cross markings, sustained serious damage, as Human Rights Watch was able to determine.[292] A fourth ambulance, belonging to the Secours Populaire Libanais hospital in Habboush near Nabatiyeh, was reported hit by small arms fire near the Kafr Ruman-Nabatiyeh junction on Tuesday, July 27.[293] A fifth ambulance was fired at by an Israeli helicopter in the village of al-Qleileh, as it was evacuating wounded civilians (see the section on civilian casualties above).

On several occasions, the Lebanese Red Cross and other recognized relief agencies were rebuffed when they requested permission from the SLA's headquarters in Marja'iyoun in the Israeli-occupied area to evacuate civilians from villages. Sometimes when permission was granted, the time given was not sufficient to do the job. A person from Kafr Ruman working at the Secours Populaire Libanais hospital in Habboush reported:

> The telephone lines were cut on Wednesday. After that, young men had to walk at night to relay news, for example of injured people. It is about one and a half hours walking from the

---

[291] Human Rights Watch interviews with the head of an international relief agency, Beirut, October 19, 1993, and with a medical officer, Tibnin, October 28, 1993. In the case of the Da'meh attack, the fact that the ambulance was clearly marked should have enabled the pilot of the attacking helicopter to identify it and compelled him to pursue his military objective without endangering the ambulance.

[292] Human Rights Watch interview, Kafra, October 28, 1993.

[293] Human Rights Watch interview with hospital staff, Habboush, Lebanon, October 22, 1993. A possible sixth ambulance was reported to have been attacked by a helicopter as it was moving a man injured in an earlier attack near the village of Ein al-Tineh in the western Beqa' valley. The wounded man was killed and three paramedics were injured in the attack. "Raid Results in 14 Killed," Voice of Lebanon, July 28, 1993, in FBIS-NES-93-143, July 28, 1993, p. 37.

center of the village [Kafr Ruman] to the Secours, going through the fields. With a car, it would take only ten minutes. The shells were falling everywhere, even in the fields, at a rate of twenty to thirty a minute.

On Wednesday, around midnight, when I was in the hospital, we received news that there was an injured person in the center of Kafr Ruman. The Lebanese Red Cross asked for and received permission from the SLA to go into the village for five minutes and evacuate that person by car. But they didn't manage to. Two hours later, the person arrived at the Kafr Ruman-Nabatiyeh junction here; he had been carried out of the village on foot. He had shrapnel wounds to the arm and leg, and we fixed him up. His name is Yahya Hamzeh; he had been fired at from the SLA position as he was walking outside.[294]

When questioned by Human Rights Watch as to the existence of a policy of blocking the population's access to relief by ordering all vehicles off the roads on pain of attack, the IDF denied ever having targeted civilian vehicles, including ambulances, traveling on roads in southern Lebanon.[295] Hospitals, ambulances and medical personnel are expressly protected in the Geneva Conventions of 1949.

Physical Damage
One express aim of Operation Accountability was to punish the inhabitants of southern Lebanon for Hizballah's activities. For example, Gen. Yehosh Dorfman, quoted above, also told the *New York Times* on July 28: "Now we are at the stage in which we are firing into the villages in order to cause

---

[294] Human Rights Watch interview, Kafr Ruman, October 31, 1993.

[295] Col. Ahaz Ben-Ari, head of the IDF's international law branch, in a communication to Human Rights Watch, May 18, 1994, said: "[O]bjects of purely civilian use, such as ambulances, wounded persons being loaded into them and cemetaries [sic] were *at no stage* targeted." (Emphasis in original).

damage to property."[296]   Article 75(2)(d) of Protocol I prohibits collective punishment at any time and in any place whatsoever.

The extensive nature of the damage sustained in numerous southern Lebanese villages confirms the IDF's declared intent. Human Rights Watch has found that in addition to the large number of civilian homes damaged, the basic infrastructure of many villages had been targeted and destroyed. By the end of Operation Accountability, conservative damage estimates suggested that some 1,000 houses had been totally destroyed, 1,500 houses had been partially destroyed, and 15,000 houses had sustained light damage.[297] Certain villages such as Jibshit suffered more than others depending on their proximity to the frontline.

In Human Rights Watch's estimation, about 120 villages close to the front line were directly or indirectly targeted. On the basis of our on-site investigation, these villages can be subdivided into three groups: (1) villages that sustained extensive damage from bombing and shelling; (2) villages that displayed moderate bomb and/or shell damage; and (3) villages that were not directly targeted but whose environs were shelled in an apparent effort to foment a refugee flow.

Category 1 encompasses nineteen villages, mostly along the front line facing Israeli-occupied territory. Here damage was extensive and exhibited the following pattern:

- one or more clusters of homes completely destroyed in air bombardments.
- several quarters or areas of the village very badly damaged by shell fire, leading to the total destruction of some homes.
- most other homes scarred by shrapnel from shell fire.

---

[296] Chris Hedges, "Israel Keeps Pounding South Lebanon," *New York Times*, July 29, 1993.

[297] Lebanese NGO Forum, "Humanitarian Situation: Review and Progress Report on South Lebanon," January 1994, p. 5. The report quotes figures of Jan Eliasson, U.N. undersecretary for humanitarian affairs, who made a three-day visit to Lebanon on August 14-17 1993. Michel Smaha, the Lebanese minister of information, claimed that an estimated 30,000 homes had been either destroyed or damaged. "Discusses Losses, Reconstruction Plan," in FBIS-NES-93-146, August 2, 1993, p. 61. Hizballah has claimed that 655 homes were totally destroyed, while 200 others were so badly damaged as to be uninhabitable. In addition, Hizballah has said that the party was instrumental in the repair of 1,800 homes that had been partially destroyed. Human Rights Watch interview with Hassan Hoballah, head of Hizballah's international relations section, Beirut, October 20, 1993.

- most homes damaged by blasts, including: broken glass, blown-in doors, and displaced walls (producing cracks).

Category 2 comprises forty-six villages, both along the front line and somewhat removed from it. Here damage was less severe, exhibiting the following pattern:

- one or two homes bombed from the air and destroyed.
- a large number of homes in the village pockmarked by shrapnel from shell fire.
- general damage to homes in the form of broken windows, doors, and furniture.

Category 3 consists of fifty-five villages. Although a few shells might have landed in these villages, there was no significant damage, but there was extensive breakage as a result of sonic booms.

Moreover, some damage occurred in residential areas close to sites targeted for their purported military nature in towns or Palestinian refugee camps further away from the front line. For example, houses were damaged in the Ein al-Hilweh refugee camp, as well as in the towns of Sidon and Tyre.

Most of the serious damage to homes in the villages in the south was due to direct targeting from the air, not to shell fire. In the village of Jibshit, for example, some fifty homes were completely destroyed, all but two of these from the air.[298] Similarly, in the village of Jarju', in the Iqlim al-Tuffah, some fifty homes were totally destroyed, mostly from the air, while 125 homes were partially destroyed, mainly from shell fire.[299]

Artillery shelling heavily damaged the village infrastructure. Not one village visited by Human Rights Watch had electricity after July 26, the second day of the attack, according to residents. The same was true for telephone lines

---

[298] Human Rights Watch interview with a local Hizballah leader, Jibshit, October 24, 1993. The same man also claimed that the vast majority of these fifty homes "belong to people who are not members of Hizballah, nor have any relation with the party through family or otherwise." An additional 320 houses in the village were partially destroyed in the attack, according to another local Hizballah official interviewed by Human Rights Watch. Jibshit has long been known as a village with numerous Hizballah officials amidst its population, and it has been the target of Israeli attacks, several of them with civilian fatalities, on occasions prior to Operation Accountability.

[299] Human Rights Watch interview with a resident, Jarju', October 26, 1993.

and all communications were down for weeks. As for water, continued supply depended on the source. If the water was piped in, the flow was invariably interrupted during the attack; if it was derived from local wells, usually there was no problem; and in one village that acquired its water from a town in the occupied area, villagers said the tap was turned off during the week of the attack.[300] According to relief sources, twenty-four water networks were damaged or destroyed during Operation Accountability, and a report to the High Relief Commission estimated that it would cost $1.57 million to repair the roads in fifty-two villages in southern Lebanon.[301] Even at the end of October 1993 there were still numerous signs of shell impact on roads leading in and out of villages.

As Human Rights Watch was able to observe, many cemeteries, mosques, churches and schools were damaged in the assault. The Lebanese ministry of education reported that a total of fifty-three schools had sustained damage.[302] At the time of the Human Rights Watch mission, primary-school children were still taking classes inside the bombed-out shell of their school in Kafra. Damage to cemeteries in numerous villages in the south also raises serious questions about Israel's intent during the seven-day campaign. Human Rights Watch, which visited a total of twenty-one Lebanese villages in 1993, surveyed destruction to eleven cemeteries in Shukin, Zawtar al-Sharqiyeh, Jibshit, Kafr Malki, Jba'a, Ein Biswar, Zabqin, Kafra, Kafr Ruman, Jarju', and Khirbet Silm. The graveyards of Jibshit and Khirbet Silm were clearly hit by numerous shells. In Jibshit, in a rather peculiar retroactive punishment, the grave of a Hizballah leader killed by Israeli forces in 1983, Sheikh Ghareb Harb, was reported to have been rocketed by a helicopter; the damage observed there suggested precise targeting.

International norms have long prohibited the unnecessary destruction of property. The 1907 Hague Conventions, which have entered into customary international law and have been accepted by Israel as such, forbid the destruction

---

[300] This was the case with the village of Qabrikha, which obtains its water from the village of Taibeh in the occupied zone. The water reportedly comes in for six hours twice weekly, but during the week of the campaign, no water was piped in. Human Rights Watch interview with a resident, Qabrikha, October 30, 1993.

[301] Cited in Lebanese NGO Forum, "Humanitarian Situation," p. 5.

[302] Lebanese Ministry of Education, cited in ibid., p. 4.

of property unless there are "imperatives demanded by the necessity of war."[303] Article 52(1) of Protocol I also expressly demands that "civilian objects shall not be the object of attack or of reprisals."

Hizballah Rocket Attacks

In the escalation of tensions leading up to Operation Accountability, Hizballah had launched several Katyusha attacks, including one on Friday, July 23 that apparently triggered Israel's decision to begin the operation. Israel claims that during the week of fighting, Hizballah fired 151 rockets into northern Israel and 122 into southern Lebanon.[304] Two civilians were killed and twenty-four injured as a result of these rocket attacks in Israel.

The first Katyusha attacks of the seven-day conflict came in the afternoon of Sunday, July 25, the first day of Operation Accountability. The IDF reported fifty rockets were fired into northern Israel and southern Lebanon that day. During the week of fighting, Hizballah fired Katyusha rockets at targets all along the Israel-Lebanon border, with a concentration in the upper northeast near Kiryat Shemona.[305] Locations in Israeli-occupied southern Lebanon were also attacked. It appears that Katyushas were fired randomly and sporadically at most target locations—once a day, twice a day, every other day, usually in volleys of just one, two, or three rockets at a time.

One Israeli summed up the situation: "Rockets fell across the whole of northern Israel. A population of tens of thousands was pinned down for a week. The sporadic nature of the attacks made it perhaps even more traumatic: God knows when, God knows where they will fall next."[306]

---

[303] Article 23(g) of The Hague Convention IV, 1907.

[304] Col. Ahaz Ben-Ari, head of the IDF's international law branch, in a communication to Human Rights Watch, May 18, 1994.

[305] Human Rights Watch visited twelve locations in northern Israel that were attacked during Operation Accountability. Seven were in northeast Israel (the Galilee panhandle) where rocket attacks were heaviest: Kiryat Shemona, Metulla, Kefar Yuval, Misgav'am, Margaliyot, Menara, and Kefar Blum. Two were in north-central Israel: Alma and Hurfeish. Three were in northwest Israel: Shelomi, Gesher HaZiv, and Nahariya. Other locations that reportedly came under attack include Yiftah in the northeast, Dishon, Adamit, Shomera, and Ma'alot in the north-central area, and Liman and Sa'ar in the northwest.

[306] Human Rights Watch interview, Nahariya, November 21, 1993.

Hizballah's stated objective was to inflict civilian casualties and damage, thereby causing Israel to halt its air and artillery attacks.[307] Yet, the Katyushas caused strikingly few injuries and little property damage. In only a small number of locations did the rockets actually fall within the populated area of a village or kibbutz; they usually hit in adjacent fields or orchards. There were no military deaths or injuries from Katyusha fire in Israel. As far as could be determined, no military installations were hit. However, the economic impact of the rocket attacks was significant in terms of loss of business in the north, as much of the population fled south and many stores closed down.

Despite the relatively little damage, it is clear that the Katyusha attacks terrorized the civilian population in northern Israel. Tens of thousands of people fled to the south. Most people who remained were confined to community shelters or private "security rooms" for long periods of time. In some locations, women and children spent nearly twenty-four hours a day for a solid week in shelters, while men would come out only to perform essential tasks, such as feeding animals.

While the "kill radius" of a single-round Katyusha rocket is small, a volley of forty rockets is clearly able to cover a large area. As employed by Hizballah in northern Israel, the Katyushas have had an indiscriminate effect, and their use by Hizballah therefore clearly violates the injunction against indiscriminate attacks in Article 51 of Protocol I. Although Hizballah rocket attacks on populated areas in Israel were much smaller in scale than Israeli artillery and air attacks on villages in southern Lebanon, Hizballah was guilty of many of the same violations of the laws of war:[308]

- Deliberate targeting of civilians and civilian property, and failure to distinguish between civilian population and combatants: Hizballah admitted this was the case.
- Failure to protect the civilian population: Hizballah issued no warnings of its attacks.

---

[307] Hassan Hoballah, head of the international relations section of Hizballah's political bureau, told Human Rights Watch: "Israel targeted civilians and we responded. We fired at Israeli settlements to press them to stop the shelling." Interview, Beirut, October 20, 1993.

[308] As one observer put it, "Everybody was shooting indiscriminately, but Israel had more firepower." Telephone interview with Martin Kramer, Dayan Center, Tel Aviv University, November 18, 1993.

- Indiscriminate attacks: The obvious lack of accuracy indicates the indiscriminate nature of the Hizballah attacks.
- Use of weapons to terrorize the civilian population: The sporadic, non-intensive nature of the attacks indicates that they were intended to terrorize, not to accomplish a military objective.
- Attacks against civilians by way of reprisals: Hizballah justified its attacks as retaliation for Israeli attacks in southern Lebanon.

Kiryat Shemona

Kiryat Shemona, with a population of some 15,000, was widely reported to have suffered the most from Katyusha attacks. A local official told Human Rights Watch that forty rockets fell inside the town during the week, with an unknown number landing in the surrounding mountains and areas.[309] Two civilians were killed, and eleven were injured. Four buildings were hit, all private houses or apartments. An Israeli army installation known as Post 769 is located at the edge of the city, but it was not hit.

There were no warnings from Hizballah of pending rocket attacks, though everyone was aware that a possible attack was imminent. The mayor had instructed citizens to leave the city and on Sunday, July 25, the first day of Operation Accountability, 600 children and 500 elderly people were bused out. By Wednesday, about half the city had departed, mostly via their own cars.[310]

The two deaths occurred in separate rocket attacks on Sunday evening. One victim, a 33-year-old father of three, had gone out to buy cigarettes and was killed when a Katyusha landed in the street nearby. The location was a strictly residential neighborhood, near downtown. The military base was about three kilometers away. Another Katyusha landed nearly simultaneously about two kilometers away and killed a 24-year-old man as it hit the front porch of his house.

Additional attacks took place on Tuesday, Wednesday, Thursday, and Saturday. The attacks came at all times of day—morning, afternoon, and night. Kiryat Shemona became a ghost town for the week; most people left and those who remained stayed in shelters, many for twenty-four hours a day. People came out of the shelters about 7:00 p.m. on Saturday, after the Israeli Army said it was safe.

---

[309] Human Rights Watch interview with Yoram Eventsur, spokesman for the office of the mayor, Kiryat Shemona, November 19, 1993.

[310] Ibid. Others estimated that 80-90 percent of residents left the town.

Menara

Menara is a kibbutz of about 350 people right on the border with Israel. Residents said that about twenty Katyushas landed on Menara property, damaging apple orchards, but none struck buildings or people. Two nearby Israeli military bases were not hit. Rockets landed day and night. The kibbutz received no warnings from Hizballah. Most women and children stayed in bomb shelters the entire week. Men worked during the day. Few people left the kibbutz to go further south.[311]

Mickey Bar-On, a 29-year-old resident of Menara, said that the Israeli forces were shooting artillery nearly twenty-four hours a day, but that when they paused for an hour or so, Katyusha attacks would increase. He said, "If you hear a noise, then a whistle, it's ours. If you hear a whistle, then a noise, it's a Katyusha." Mr. Bar-On said, "If someone says he is not afraid, he is the biggest liar on earth. Everyone is afraid. Going to work during the day is not brave. You try to maintain life. You don't feel like something special. Chickens have to be fed. They don't care if there is a war. Apples have to be watered. I hope it won't happen again. We've had enough."[312]

Metulla

Metulla is a town of some 2,000 people located north of Kiryat Shemona, close to the border. According to a spokesperson from the office of the mayor, Metulla had been hit by Katyushas in 1979, 1985, and 1990, and the government had built shelters for residents. The spokesperson said that about sixty rockets fell around Metulla during Operation Accountability, but none landed in the town.[313] Most fell into the surrounding fields, causing minor property damage to irrigation systems and farmers' trees. Several military compounds are located inside the town, including one directly adjacent to the shopping center and grocery store.

There were no warnings from Hizballah, but the IDF warned people on Sunday to prepare to leave. A majority of the town's population left for the south, including most women and children. Most people slept in shelters, and some people stayed in shelters all day. The rocket attacks occurred at different

---

[311] Human Rights Watch interview, Menara, November 20, 1993.

[312] Ibid.

[313] Human Rights Watch interview with Clery Lishansky, Metulla, November 19, 1993.

times of day and night; sometimes a single rocket would land, at other times five or six. Said one resident, "You sit and wait and never know."

The spokesperson said that Israeli aircraft and artillery made endless, extremely loud noise all week long: "It was continuous, twenty-four hours a day all week long, every second of the day. It got a little better Thursday night, Friday and Saturday. You had to shout to be heard, even indoors."[314]

Other Civilian Targets

Nahariya is a major resort town on the northwest coast, with a population of about 45,000. It had been the target of rocket attacks in the past. While no Katyushas landed inside the town during Operation Accountability, some fell close by in surrounding areas. Most residents did not evacuate and head south, although in the case of some families, women and children left the area. Most of those who stayed kept indoors during the day and slept in shelters. Many businesses shut down for the entire week, causing economic hardship at the peak time of tourist season.[315]

In Kefar Yuval, a cooperative village of about 350, a man said Katyushas fell only on one day, landing in the fields and causing no damage. He said people ignored the Army's instructions to go into the shelters, because the shelters have no electricity or toilets. He said it had been "no problem," but his wife disagreed: "It's impossible to live like this. There is fear. It's frightening. You don't know when things will fall."[316]

A worker in a field in Margaliyot, a cooperative village of about 350, said that eight Katyushas fell during the week, but that none landed inside the village. He noted, "The children can now tell the difference between the noise of a Katyusha and the noise of Israeli artillery."[317]

In Shelomi, a rocket landed ten meters from a civilian warehouse with about sixty workers inside. Residents said that many people went south, and that

---

[314] Ibid.

[315] Human Rights Watch interviews, Nahariya, November 20-21, 1993.

[316] Human Rights Watch interview, Kefar Yuval, November 20, 1993.

[317] Human Rights Watch interview, Margaliyot, November 20, 1993.

most of those who remained did not work, but went into the shelters. There are military bases nearby, both to the north and west.[318]

In Kefar Blum, residents said that about a dozen Katyushas fell during the week. Most landed near a concert center and some people thought it was purposefully targeted because it draws large crowds in the summer. While few evacuated, many people stayed in shelters or private security rooms all week. One resident said that Katyushas don't cause much damage, but are an effective "weapon of terror" against civilians.[319]

David, aged thirty-five, was injured when a Katyusha hit the sheep barn twenty yards behind his house in the cooperative village of Alma. Two other men were slightly injured and forty-nine sheep were killed. The attack came on Sunday, the first day of Operation Accountability. There were no further attacks during the week, but women and children spent most of the time in shelters.[320]

Human Rights Watch has not received any reports of civilian casualties in the Israeli-occupied zone during Operation Accountability. Yet Hizballah appears to have fired a number of Katyushas at populated areas inside the zone. Apparently one of the main targets in Israeli-occupied zone in southern Lebanon was the town of Marja'iyoun. One local Lebanese resident, Noel, said that forty Katyushas fell in and around the town during what she described as "a week of terror." She said that rockets landed every day, but at different times, and that people were very afraid. Schools were closed and most people stayed inside in secure rooms. Noel said that houses, a Catholic school, an Eastern Catholic Church and a social hall were hit. She was unaware of any civilian casualties. She said that there is an IDF/SLA military camp, with perhaps 2,000 soldiers, about one kilometer from the town.[321]

Aftermath of Operation Accountability

The intense fighting ended with a cease-fire in the evening of Saturday, July 31, but the situation quickly reverted to the status quo ante. Less than three weeks after the cease-fire Hizballah guerrillas killed eight Israeli soldiers in the

---

[318] Human Rights Watch interview, Shelomi, November 20, 1993. A girl of about six imitated a rocket's whistling noise when she heard the word "Katyusha."

[319] Human Rights Watch interview, Kefar Blum, November 19, 1993.

[320] Human Rights Watch interview, Alma, November 20, 1993.

[321] Human Rights Watch interview, Metulla, November 20, 1993.

Israeli-occupied area.[322]   Then, on September 14, two Lebanese civilians were killed by IDF/SLA shelling after earlier guerrilla attacks on Israeli forces.

The following is a short chronology of clashes back and forth between the IDF/SLA, on one side, and Hizballah and other guerrilla groups, on the other, since Operation Accountability, and reports of civilian casualties, to show the on-going nature of the fighting and the instability inherent in the July 1993 understandings. This chronology is based on press accounts and is not meant to be comprehensive.

1993

August 19 - Hizballah kills eight IDF soldiers and wounds four more in two attacks in the Israeli-occupied area.

September 14 - In six attacks Hizballah wounds one Israeli soldier and five SLA militiamen. IDF/SLA retaliatory artillery and mortar shelling kills two civilians in southern Lebanon.

1994

February 7 - Hizballah kills four IDF soldiers and wounds five others in the occupied zone. Israel attacks several villages in southern Lebanon in retaliation. Hizballah fires twenty-two Katayusha rockets into the town of Marja'iyoun in the occupied zone.

March 7 - Seven SLA militiamen are killed and fourteen wounded in fighting in the Israeli-occupied zone. Two civilians are killed in the crossfire, and the Israeli retaliation wounds an eight-year-old girl in a village in the Iqlim al-Tuffah.

June 1 - The IAF attacks a Hizballah base in the Beq'a valley, killing some thirty alleged Hizballah members and wounding about eighty others (mostly teenagers). Hizballah fires retaliatory rockets into Israel. Following repeated clashes, Israel moves tanks and artillery up to the Israel-Lebanon border on June 3.

June 20 - One Israeli soldier is killed and three are wounded in a Hizballah ambush. Israeli retaliatory shelling kills an elderly woman and wounds three other civilians in Kafr Tibnit. Hizballah shells the town of Marja'iyoun in the occupied area in response. A sixteen-year-old girl is wounded by Israeli shelling of Nabatiyeh on June 21.

---

[322] Clyde Habe:man, "Bomb Kills 8 Israeli Soldiers On Patrol in South Lebanon," *New York Times*, August 20, 1993.

August 4 - An IAF missile kills six civilians and injures seventeen others in the village of Deir al-Zahrani. Israel apologizes. Hizballah fires rockets at northern Israel in retaliation. No casualties are reported.

August 6 - Hizballah attack kills two IDF soldiers and wounds at least two others across the front line from Arab Salim in the occupied area.

September 8 - An IDF soldier is killed and another wounded in a Hizballah attack near Tallousa in the occupied area.

October 19 - IDF flechette-filled shells kill four civilians and wound four more in Nabatiyeh al-Fowqa. Hizballah fires rockets into Israel in retaliation. Israel shells areas in southern Lebanon in response.

December 8 - Nine SLA militiamen are killed in a Hizballah ambush in the occupied area. Israel responds with artillery, airplane and helicopter attacks on southern Lebanon.

1995

February 19 - Hizballah guerrillas attack SLA and IDF positions in the occupied area. The SLA/IDF retaliate with a shelling barrage, killing two civilians and injuring four others in Kafr Ruman.

March 31 - Hizballah leader Rida' Yassin is killed in an Israeli helicopter gunship attack. In the subsequent rocket and artillery exchanges, one civilian is killed in northern Israel (the first in nearly two years), while four civilians are reported killed in southern Lebanon.

April 9 - Five SLA militiamen are killed by Hizballah guerrillas in the occupied area.

April 15 - Three SLA militiamen and one guerrilla are wounded in fighting in the occupied area. Hizballah rockets set fire to a hospital in Marja'iyoun in the occupied area.

April 20 - Three Lebanese civilians are wounded in IDF/SLA shelling.

May 4 - In IDF/SLA shelling on the village of Jarju', one civilian is killed and two others are injured. Hizballah responds by firing rockets at Kiryat Shemona, injuring three civilians.

May 30 - A twelve-year-old girl is killed and four more civilians are wounded by SLA shelling in Shaqra. Hizballah responds by firing rockets into northern Israel. No casualties are reported there.

June 17 - After guerrillas launched a rocket from an area near Kafr Tibnit, the SLA/IDF lobbed shells at the village, killing an elderly farmer as well as a number of sheep and goats.

June 22 - Israeli shells kill a young woman in the village of Shaqra. One civilian is killed and nine are wounded in a retaliatory Hizballah rocket attack on the Club Med resort in Nahariya in northern Israel.

July 8 - IDF tank-fired flechette shells kill three children and wound four others in the Lebanese town of Nabatiyeh. Hizballah responds by firing twenty-seven Katyusha rockets into northern Israel.

July 30 - One IDF soldier is killed and several wounded in a Hizballah attack in the occupied area. At least ten Lebanese civilians are wounded when a Hizballah rocket hits the village of Rihan in the Israeli-occupied area.

August 21 - SLA/IDF shells land in the village of Kafr Tibnit. No casualties are reported.

October 12 - Three IDF soldiers are killed in a Hizballah ambush in the occupied area. The IDF responds with artillery shelling of villages in southern Lebanon. No casualties are reported.

October 15 - Six IDF soldiers are killed in a Hizballah ambush near Jezzin in the SLA-controlled Jezzin salient.

October 22 - Following a guerrilla attack on IDF positions in the occupied area, machine gun fire injures a five-year-old Lebanese boy in the village of Kafr Ruman.

October 31 - Three guerrillas are killed and seven SLA militiamen are wounded in exchanges.

November 2 - Two SLA militiamen are killed and five Israeli soldiers are wounded by guerrillas in the occupied area.

November 26 - A flechette shell kills one guerrilla and wounds five others near Kafr Tibnit. Several houses in Kafr Tibnit are "peppered" with steel darts. Hizballah fires at least five volleys of Katyusha rockets into northern Israel on November 28, wounding at least eight Israeli civilians. Israel responds by shelling Lebanese villages north of the Israeli-occupied area.

December 6 - Three guerrillas and one IDF soldier are killed, and three SLA militiamen are wounded in fighting in the occupied area. IDF/SLA artillery fires dozens of shells at villages in southern Lebanon.

December 29 - Following a Hizballah mortar attack on an IDF/SLA position near the village of al-Qantara in the occupied zone, an IDF tank-fired flechette shell kills one Lebanese civilian and wounds four others in the village of Qabrikha. Hizballah retaliates with Katyusha rocket attacks on northern Israel.

1996

January 18 - One Lebanese civilian dies two days after he and another civilian are wounded by Israeli shelling of the village of Bra'ashit.

February 5 - A Lebanese woman is killed and another wounded by IDF/SLA shelling in Mansoureh. The same day a Lebanese man in the occupied area is reported wounded by guerrilla fire.

February 16 - Guerrillas fire at SLA/IDF posts in the occupied area, injuring five militiamen, as well as an Israeli soldier. Two guerrillas are killed in return fire. In retaliation for the attack, Israeli artillery shells the outskirts of twenty villages in southern Lebanon, wounding a nine-year-old girl in Kafr Tibnit.

February 26 - Two IDF soldiers are killed in the occupied area. In retaliation Israel shells south Lebanese villages.

February 27 - An SLA militiaman is killed in the occupied area.

March 4 - Four IDF soldiers are killed and nine injured in a Hizballah ambush on the Hula-Markaba road in the occupied area.

March 9 - One SLA militiaman is killed and an IDF soldier and an SLA militiaman are wounded in a Hizballah attack in the occupied area.

March 10 - Two IDF soldiers are killed in a Hizballah attack in Kafr Kila in the occupied area. Israel responds with heavy artillery fire on villages in southern Lebanon.

March 14 - Five IDF soldiers are injured in a roadside bomb and Hizballah ambush in the occupied area.

March 20 - An IDF officer and a SLA militiaman are killed by a suicide bomber in the occupied area. In retaliation, Israel shells villages in southern Lebanon. Hizballah then vows to retaliate against northern Israel if the shelling continues.

March 30 - IDF/SLA shelling kills two civilians and wounds one other in the village of Yater. Israel calls the attack a mistake. Hizballah fires two salvoes of Katyusha rockets into northern Israel in retaliation. No casualties are reported.

April 8 - A roadside explosion kills a teenage Lebanese boy and wounds three other people in the village of Bra'ashit north of the Israeli-occupied area. Hizballah blames Israel. Israel orders residents of northern Israel into air-raid shelters. At least six Israeli civilians are wounded, one seriously, in a Hizballah retaliatory rocket attack on northern Israel on April 9. That same day, Israel responds with an attack on the village of Khirbet Silm, in which two civilians are wounded. Israel threatens the residents of south Lebanon.

April 10 - An IDF soldier is killed and three are wounded in a Hizballah attack
     on their outpost in the occupied zone.

April 11 - Israel launches "Operation Grapes of Wrath" in Lebanon.

VI. QUESTIONS ABOUT SOME OF THE WEAPONS USED IN THE CONFLICT

Under international humanitarian law, states are obligated to choose their weapons according to how they will be used. If a weapon, used to defeat a military enemy, is likely to cause disproportionate civilian casualties, an alternative weapon that would not have that effect should be chosen.[323] There is no doubt that the indiscriminate shelling by Israeli forces of villages in southern Lebanon is illegal, as is the indiscriminate firing of Katyusha rockets by Hizballah into northern Israel. But in addition, Human Rights Watch is concerned that Israel has used flechette shells and phosphorus in southern Lebanon illegally. The flechette shell, because of its large "kill radius," can be particularly destructive when used in civilian areas, as it appears to have been. Phosphorus, an incendiary ordinarily used for marking purposes, may have been used in an antipersonnel mode in civilian areas. Under international humanitarian law, special provisions expressly forbid the use of incendiary weapons against civilians or civilian objects.[324] By contrast, the use by armies of incendiary weapons against military targets is not generally held to violate international law, and the

---

[323] Art. 51(4) of Protocol I states in part: "Indiscriminate attacks are prohibited. Indiscriminate attacks are:...those which employ a method or means of combat which cannot be directed at a specific military objective; or those which employ a method or means of combat the effects of which cannot be limited as required by this Protocol...."

[324] Protocol III of the 1980 Convention on Prohibitions or Restrictions on the Use of Certain Conventional Weapons which may be deemed to be Excessively Injurious or to have Indiscriminate Effects defines the term "incendiary weapon" as "any weapon or munition which is primarily designed to set fire to objects or to cause burn injury to persons through the action of flame, heat, or a combination thereof, produced by a chemical reaction of a substance delivered on the target." Protocol III prohibits the use of incendiary weapons to target civilians. Israel is not a party to this Protocol. While the convention does not prohibit the use of incendiary weapons against military objectives per se, it does limit their use if it is likely that civilians would be the victims of such an attack. See Yves Sandoz, *Prohibitions or Restrictions on the Use of Certain Conventional Weapons* (Geneva: ICRC, 1981), pp. 13-14, 31-32.

use of incendiary munitions for non-weapon purposes, such as target acquisition, is legitimate and widespread.[325]

Phosphorus

Incendiary agents are "substances which...burn with a powerful...heat-producing reaction." Unlike with explosives, the combustion in incendiaries is "sustained for a relatively long period of time (minutes instead of micro-seconds)" during which time the likelihood of igniting secondary fires in inflammable substances is increased.[326] One category of incendiary weapons is phosphorus, a munition which ignites spontaneously in air and sticks to clothing and other material. The most common type of phosphorus is white phosphorus (WP). According to military experts, white phosphorus ammunition

> can have a devastating effect if it is used in the anti-personnel role. In addition to the toxicity of the smoke, burning fragments can stick to the skin and clothing to cause severe burns, and fragments of unburnt phosphorus can become buried in wounds until they are exposed during subsequent treatment....[W]hite phosphorus is widely used in shells, mortar bombs and grenades throughout the world. This reflects not only its excellent smoke-producing qualities but also, it must be acknowledged, its secondary anti-personnel role.[327]

During the Israeli invasion of Lebanon in 1982, the Israeli shelling of villages in southern Lebanon in July 1993, and subsequent shelling attacks, there have been numerous allegations of Israeli forces using phosphorus against

---

[325] There has been considerable argument over the years that incendiary weapons be banned as causing "unnecessary suffering," but proposals to ban these weapons have not met with international consensus. See Guenter Lewy, *America in Vietnam* (New York: Oxford University Press, 1978), pp. 245-48, citing Stockholm International Peace Research Institute (SIPRI), *Incendiary Weapons* (Cambridge, MA: The MIT Press, 1975), pp. 69-73, 83-86.

[326] SIPRI, *Incendiary Weapons*, p. 87.

[327] P.R. Courtney-Green, *Ammunition for the Land Battle* (London: Brassey's Ltd., 1991), pp. 195-96. See also, SIPRI *Incendiary Weapons*, pp. 98-100.

civilians.[328]   The available circumstantial evidence of the illegal use of phosphorus, and/or other incendiaries, by Israel against Lebanese civilians during the 1993 events and afterwards is so compelling as to warrant serious investigation and a public response by the Israeli government. The evidence reviewed by Human Rights Watch includes: empty artillery shells, or fragments of artillery shells, with headstamps indicating they had contained phosphorus; eyewitness testimonies of shell attacks which caused what were said to be phosphorus burns; injuries on victims that were consistent with phosphorus burns; hospital reports of treatment of burn injuries consistent with phosphorus burns; doctors' testimonies of the treatment of what they said were phosphorus burns; an Israeli press report about the use by Israeli forces in Lebanon of phosphorus as a weapon; and other reports of Israel's alleged use of phosphorus as a weapon in Lebanon.

During research on the July 1993 events, Human Rights Watch obtained testimonies on three incidents in which the use of phosphorus was alleged. Two of these occurred during daylight, the third at night time. It is assumed that daytime use of white phosphorus as a flare or marker is not justified, because smoke would be most effective during the day, whereas white phosphorus is most effective after dark.

The first of these incidents occurred in the village of Kafr Ruman, on the outskirts of Nabatiyeh just underneath SLA/IDF positions, on Monday, July 26. At about four o'clock in the afternoon, Leila Hassan Aloush, 45, decided to walk the short distance from her family's home to the home of a relative, Munifa Ali Saleh, 51, during a brief lull in the shelling, which had been continuous for most of the day. According to Aloush, she was going down the stairs into the basement of her relative's house, where the whole family had gathered: "At that point, a shell fell near our house, but everybody there was inside the shelter [basement], so no one was hurt. Then a second shell fell near the shelter [basement] that I was just entering. There was an explosion and then smoke: yellow, green, red and black, and then a big flame. I began to choke, and received burns to both my arms and my back. These are not normal burns, but phosphorus burns. My cousin Munifa suffered similar burns, but not as severely. I was taken to the Secours Libanais hospital, where I stayed nine days. Then I was transferred to

---

[328] For example, see Robert Fisk, "Israel's Proxy Army Runs 'Out of Control,'" *Independent*, July 30, 1993.

the Greek Orthodox hospital in Beirut. The doctors have told me that I will need to undergo plastic surgery on my right arm."[329]

Human Rights Watch was able to ascertain that both women suffered burns to their hands, arms and back. A surgeon at the nearby Secours Populaire Libanais hospital, interviewed separately, claimed he and his colleagues had treated nineteen cases of phosphorus burns during the fourth week of July, including Leila Aloush and Munifa Saleh. In those two particular cases, he said, "we removed the phosphorus from the women's skin with pincers. Phosphorus is crystalline and lights up." He said that phosphorus was used by Israeli forces "to scare people," and that it had mostly been used on Monday, July 26.[330]

Doctors at the Secours Populaire Libanais were unable to produce surgical records for the two women, but post-surgery medical records indicate that Leila Aloush, a diabetic, received steroids for breathing difficulties immediately after the surgery, as well as antibiotics for first and second degree burns to the face and hands. On the fourth day after admission, she also received a heavy dose of pain killers. The treatment of Munifa Saleh was very similar.[331] Independent analysis by a medical specialist in the U.S. suggests that, in the absence of surgical records, no definitive conclusions can be drawn about the exact nature of the burns, but that the medical records are not inconsistent with the type of deep burns that phosphorus can cause. The use of steroids as a prophylactic, while inappropriate in the case of serious burns, is justified if the burn injuries are confined and accompanied by another indication, like breathing difficulties. The problems in breathing are likely to have been caused by smoke inhalation at close proximity to the source of the smoke or flash. Moreover, Ms. Aloush's burns were in exposed areas (her arms and face), suggesting that the burns may have been caused by a flash from which Ms. Aloush tried to protect her face with her hands. The use of painkillers four days after the event suggests nerve damage as a result of a deep burn. Pictures of Ms. Aloush's injuries show a dark red spot on her arm, which is reminiscent of a deep burn. This might have been caused by phosphorus and is not likely to have been caused by a regular

---

[329] Human Rights Watch interview, Kafr Ruman, October 22, 1993.

[330] Human Rights Watch interview with Dr. Ahmad Mushawrab, program director and general surgeon, Hikmat al-Amin Hospital of the Secours Populaire Libanais, Habboush (Nabatiyeh), October 22, 1993.

[331] Medical records, file #9986 (Munifa Saleh) and file #9987 (Leila Aloush Saleh), Hospital of the Secours Populaire Libanais, Nabatiyeh.

flash burn. The fact that no ointments were used on the wounds also suggests that the burns must have been very serious. In sum, according to the analyst, the treatment which Ms. Aloush and Ms. Saleh received is consistent with smoke inhalation and deep burns, including burns caused by phosphorus, but it is not possible to tell from available hospital records whether or not the burns were actually caused by phosphorus.[332]

Ms. Aloush showed Human Rights Watch the fragments of a shell which, she claimed, was from the July 1993 attack. After cleaning the fragment, which was the base part of a 155mm artillery shell, Human Rights Watch discovered the following headstamp: RM 0-2-118 1957 155MM M110, which is a standard U.S. designation. The code RM 0-2-118 1957 suggests that the shell was probably made in France or Germany in 1957, while the code M110 indicates that the shell is most likely to have contained white phosphorus.[333]

The second case allegedly involving the use of phosphorus and investigated by Human Rights Watch concerns a family in the village of Haris, on the border of the Israeli-occupied zone. The family of seven (Hassan Dimashq, his wife, and five children) had arrived in Lebanon in February 1993 from a seventeen-year stay in Sierra Leone, where they had been displaced by civil war and had lost everything they owned. In Haris, they moved into the house of Hassan Dimashq's elderly father in the center of the village. At 9:30 p.m. on Monday, July 26, according to Mr. Dimashq,

> the children were asleep. There had been shelling on Sunday and Monday, but only on the outskirts of the village. We never heard any warnings. All of the people of the village were still there; no one had left. At around 5 that afternoon, the houses of the villages itself were being targeted, and so we couldn't go out anymore. We thought we were safe from the shelling

---

[332] Human Rights Watch interview with Dr. David A. Flockhart, M.D., Ph.D., Assistant Professor of Medicine and Pharmacology, Georgetown University Medical Center, Washington, DC, August 11 and 17, 1994.

[333] The information about the meaning of the code was obtained from Bob Leiendecker and Richard Buckley, National Ground Intelligence Center. (Interview, Charlottesville, VA, October 31, 1994). For the designations M107, M110, and M116, see Terry J. Gander and Ian V. Hogg, editors, *Jane's Ammunition Handbook 1993-94* (Coulsdon, Surrey: Jane's Information Group Limited, 1992), pp. 195-98 on HE M107 shells; pp. 205-07 on WP M110 shells; and pp. 208-10 on Smoke M116 shells.

because the house is in the heart of the village and is not
exposed.

My three youngest children were asleep on the double bed in
the bedroom inside. At 9:30 we heard a strong explosion not
very far off. I immediately went to check on the three children
to see if they had woken up from the explosion but they were
still asleep. As I left the bedroom to return to my wife and two
oldest children, a shell came through the ceiling and exploded
in the middle of the bedroom. I fell down and was injured to
the head; I don't know how or from what. But I felt nothing;
no pain.

I got to my feet and started to look for my children. They were
not where they had been, on the double bed. There was a lot
of smoke, but no fire, at least not at first. I started searching
for them blindly, and then suddenly the house lit up, I don't
know from what. I discovered that the cupboard had fallen
over, and I heard crying underneath it. I looked and found my
seven-year-old son Muhammad underneath it. I pulled him out.
He had been badly burned and also suffered head injuries from
shrapnel. I put him over my shoulder. Then I discovered Jihad,
who was five, lying four meters further over, and I picked him
up as well. Then I discovered the little girl, Maryam, who was
three, next to the stove in the kitchen area. All three were
burned, and I carried them out into the street. About five or
ten minutes after I got out of the house, it caught fire.[334]

Both Jihad and Maryam later died from their injuries; Muhammad
recovered but was seriously scarred on one arm from burns. When Human
Rights Watch visited Haris at the end of October 1993, the house of the Dimashq
family remained in ruins. The bedroom in which the three children had been
asleep was burned out, the blackened skeleton of what had once been a bed still
standing in the middle of the room. There was a large mustard-yellow-colored
area on the wall above the front of the bed which, Mr. Dimashq asserted, had not
been there before the attack. An entry hole was visible in the roof, and two
pieces of shell were lying on the floor in the midst of the rubble. One was the

[334] Human Rights Watch interview, Haris, October 30, 1993.

base ejection plug of a shell; the other a large shell fragment. Neither bore a headstamp enabling identification, but given their size and shape, they both clearly belonged to a 155mm artillery shell, presumably the same shell. The size of the shrapnel suggests that the shell broke rather than exploded, which would make it either a smoke or phosphorus shell rather than a high-explosive (HE) shell containing TNT. The only logical conclusion, given the night-time attack, is that this was a phosphorus shell used either for illumination or as a weapon. Another possibility is that this was an HE round with a low-order detonation (explaining the uncharacteristically large pieces of shrapnel) that produced smoke and a flash burn on the three children. The evidence available on the scene of the attack, while inconclusive, is not inconsistent with, and even suggestive of, an attack with a phosphorus shell.

Both local medical staff who saw the children before they were transferred to Beirut and international humanitarian officials who visited the scene of the attack asserted that the Haris family had been the target of a phosphorus attack.[335] A doctor who treated the Dimashq children within twenty-fours hours of the attack said that, while he was unable to make a positive identification of the cause of the burns, he could "not exclude the possibility of the use of phosphorus."[336] An independent medical expert has commented that the sequence of events—first a flash, then smoke, then fire—was consistent with the use of phosphorus, but he was unable to evaluate either the shrapnel or the photographs of the scene and burns on the surviving boy.[337]

The third case involved a rare shelling attack on a position of the Lebanese Army in a village at some distance from the occupied zone. Israeli/SLA gunners had been targeting alleged Hizballah positions, and villages along the border of the occupied zone generally, during the July 1993 assault, but had been avoiding shelling Lebanese Army positions. In this case, however, nine artillery shells were fired at the village of Kafr Hatta on the road from Sidon to villages in the Iqlim al-Tuffah, where a unit of the Lebanese Army's Fifth Brigade had dug itself in. Kafr Hatta itself suffered no shell damage during that

---

[335] Neither wished to be quoted on the record.

[336] Human Rights Watch interview with Dr. Nimri Mal'ab, plastic surgeon, American University Hospital, Beirut, October 31, 1993.

[337] Human Rights Watch interview with Dr. David A. Flockhart, M.D., Ph.D., Assistant Professor of Medicine and Pharmacology, Georgetown University Medical Center, Washington, DC, August 11 and 17, 1994.

week, except during that single attack, at 10 a.m. on July 27, in which four civilians were injured. According to a resident of a neighboring village, the Israeli/SLA shelling came in response to four shells being fired by the Lebanese army gunners in Kafr Hatta at an IDF/SLA position near the village of Sujud in the Jezzin salient a little while earlier.[338] A Lebanese officer present at the scene at the time of the attack confirmed the shelling by both sides (claiming that his unit opened fire "because all our units were under fire") and said that he had collected fragments from high-explosive shells (HE/M107) as well as phosphorus shells (WP/M110), both 155mm shells fired by an M109 self-propelled howitzer. He speculated that the intended target was an ammunition store of the Lebanese Army in the village. Characteristically, the WP shell had not exploded but broke on impact.[339]

In the view of Human Rights Watch, the above cases offer testimony of the use by Israeli forces of shells containing either white phosphorus and/or other incendiary munitions against villages in southern Lebanon. We received several other reports of the use of phosphorus during the July 1993 events, and collected additional pieces of shrapnel that bore headstamps indicating the shells were phosphorus rounds. Intriguingly, the political correspondent of the Israel Television Network (ITN) in Jerusalem, Gabi Sukenik, basing himself on senior Israeli government sources, reported on July 26 that during the "third stage" of the operation that day, "the IDF started shelling terrorist targets inside some of the south Lebanon villages with smoke and phosphorous shells."[340] When

---

[338] Human Rights Watch interview, Kafr Malki, October 25, 1993.

[339] Human Rights Watch interview, Beirut, October 26, 1993. The IDF has not offered a direct response to the question whether positions of the Lebanese Army were shelled. According to the head of the IDF's international law branch, Col. Ahaz Ben-Ari, "there would have been no justification in the targeting of Lebanese Army or United Nations positions." (Correspondence, May 18, 1994). If the Lebanese Army did have a munitions store in Kafr Hatta, it would have been in violation of the injunction to avoid locating military objectives within or near densely populated areas (Protocol I, Art. 58(b)).

[340] Foreign Information Broadcast Service, FBIS-NES-93-142, July 27, 1993, p. 24. The report, which was uncritical of Israeli government policy during the assault, described three stages in the campaign: a first stage on Sunday, July 25, that consisted of "air raids outside the villages"; a second stage in which "helicopters and tanks joined the operation in surgical bombing near Shiite villages"; and a third stage that "started with a heavier shelling of the outskirts of the villages, and was followed with warnings to the civilians that they should escape." As part of that stage of the assault, according to the

questioned by the Israeli daily *Yedi'ot Ahronot* about the IDF's reported use of phosphorus bombs, the commander of the Israeli Air Force, Maj.-Gen. Herzl Budinger, declared: "We do not use such bombs."[341] A former Israeli soldier who had served in Lebanon in the mid-1980s, told Human Rights Watch, to the contrary, that in his experience soldiers are routinely equipped with phosphorus grenades, and that phosphorus rounds are euphemistically referred to in the Israeli army as "exploding smoke" to avoid acknowledging their true identity.[342]

Repeated attempts by Human Rights Watch to elicit an official IDF comment on the IDF's alleged use of phosphorus in Lebanon have met with no response. Col. Ahaz Ben-Ari, head of the IDF's international law branch, refused to address the use of phosphorus specifically in a letter to Human Rights Watch, declaring that as long as "the threat from Hizbullah is still present, it is not unreasonable to refuse to disclose details of the specific designations of weaponry and methods and bases for their operation." He added that "the use of all weaponry by the IDF in the conduct of 'Operation Accountability' conformed to accepted standards of international law."[343]

U.S. military experts consulted on the possible use of phosphorus by Israeli forces noted the apparent high incidence of the firing of illuminating and incendiary rounds during the July 1993 artillery assault on Lebanese villages, which they deemed unusual. One possible explanation for this, in their view, was that such rounds lessen civilian casualties, and their use would therefore have made good sense in any attempt to compel people to leave their homes.[344] This is consistent with the declared objective of Israeli leaders to foment a refugee exodus from villages in southern Lebanon to Beirut. Human Rights Watch

---

reporter, smoke and phosphorus rounds were used. The reporter also anticipated a fourth stage, which was going to consist of "a heavy shelling of each settlement in which terrorists will be located."

[341] *Yedi'ot Ahronot*, July 30, 1993, in FBIS-NES-93-145, July 30, 1993, p. 32.

[342] Memo to Human Rights Watch, August 2, 1993.

[343] Correspondence, May 18, 1994. Human Rights Watch sent another letter to the IDF in September 1995 concerning allegations of the use by Israeli forces in southern Lebanon of both dart shells ("flechettes") and phosphorus shells. That letter had not been answered as of April 1996.

[344] Human Rights Watch interview with Bob Leiendecker and Richard Buckley, National Ground Intelligence Center, Charlottesville, VA, October 31, 1994.

continued to receive reports of the alleged use of phosphorus by Israeli forces in southern Lebanon in 1994 and 1995.[345] The U.S. Department of State reported that there were, "credible accounts of IDF use of phosphorous shells against military and civilian targets" in southern Lebanon in 1994.[346] During interviews in August 1995, residents of the south made repeated mention of an apparently systematic policy of burning agricultural land in areas near the Israeli-occupied area with phosphorus shells. "The Israelis are destroying houses, burning crops, forcing civilians to leave," said a farmer in Zawtar al-Sharqiyeh. "Every year, they burn the same land here. They use phosphorus shells. The smoke has a smell. They explode lightly but produce fire and a lot of smoke. Every month they use phosphorus on the fields, twenty or thirty shells each time. They do not permit us to put the fire out. They would start sniping if we did. The [Litani] river is two kilometers from the fields. They will not let anyone near the river. They say it is a military area." The farmer said that the shells are fired from the positions at Alman and Shumariyeh. He added that no one in Zawtar had been injured by phosphorus shells.[347]

Residents of the village of Shaqra also complained about the burning of agricultural lands, which has forced many families to leave the area. Referring to the IDF/SLA shelling that injured her daughter Maisa Ismail on May 30, 1995, one resident told Human Rights Watch: "Two days before my daughter's accident they burned all the wheat." She pointed to the gently sloping hillside near her house and said that this was where the attack had occurred. She said that at least twenty phosphorus shells had been dropped on the area. When asked how she and other residents knew that the shells were phosphorus, she said that, unlike other

---

[345] There have been numerous allegations of the use of phosphorus shells in southern Lebanon in this period. See for example, "Lebanese Radio Reports "Ferocious" Clashes, Two Days of Israeli Shelling," Voice of Lebanon, BBC Monitoring Service: Middle East, October 31, 1994. On June 13, 1995, UNIFIL issued a protest to the IDF for the deliberate firing, apparently by the SLA, of phosphorus shells toward local crops in southern Lebanon. Human Rights Watch telephone interview with a UNIFIL spokesman, November 20, 1995.

[346] U.S. Department of State, *Country Reports on Human Rights Practices for 1993* (Washington, DC, 1994), p. 1236.

[347] Human Rights Watch interview, Zawtar al-Sharqiyeh, August 23, 1995. The same witness was quoted in chapter 4 above.

shells, these burned when they hit the ground. The shells had come down over a period of two hours, the witness said.[348]

Flechettes

Human Rights Watch also has questions about the IDF's use of flechette, or dart, shells in civilian areas in southern Lebanon. A flechette shell is an antipersonnel weapon that contains ten to fourteen thousand 1.5-inch steel darts which, as they are released from the canister, spread out in an arc that can reach a maximum width of about ninety-four yards.[349] The IDF has reportedly used tank-fired shells filled with flechettes in southern Lebanon for many years, but especially in the last two years there have been repeated reports of deaths and injuries from flechettes.

The IDF has been using flechette munitions, rather than other tank-fired antipersonnel shells, in southern Lebanon mainly for their ability to penetrate dense foliage. Conventional antipersonnel shells are filled with steel balls or slugs which, unlike flechettes, are quickly slowed to non-wounding velocity by vegetation. There has been research to increase the wounding potential of flechettes (through different materials and design), but innovations arising from such research do not appear to have been incorporated into the Israeli flechette munitions, possibly because of cost or packing problems. The tank-fired shell is the only large line-of-sight antipersonnel munition fielded by Israel in southern Lebanon. Israel does have aircraft, rocket, and artillery cluster munitions, but these have not been fielded on the perimeter of the Israeli-occupied area, and are not as easily targeted. Furthermore, the Israeli use of cluster munitions during the 1982 invasion of Lebanon was condemned by the international community and led to a U.S. suspension of cluster weapon sales to Israel. Since then there has been no evidence to indicate that cluster munitions other than flechette shells have been used by Israel in Lebanon.[350]

---

[348] Human Rights Watch interview, Shaqra, August 18, 1995. The case is described in more detail in the section on recent violations above.

[349] Jane's Information Group, *Jane's Ammunition Handbook 1993-94* (Surrey: Jane's Information Group Limited, 1992), p. 134.

[350] Companies in the U.S. have advertised flechette shells in their catalogues. Two examples in 1996:

FIREQUEST INTERNATIONAL, INC.

According to UNIFIL, the IDF in southern Lebanon has two types of tank-fired flechette shells. One is a 105mm caliber shell, apparently for use by the Merkava I and II tank, and the other is a 120mm caliber shell for use by the newer Merkava III tank.[351] The Finnish UNIFIL Battalion recovered one fuze for a flechette shell near Deir Siriyan in late 1995. The markings were: 1976 HAT 1-10, Range in meters x 100, [illegible]...ZE MTM571. The MTM 571 is a U.S.

---

218 East First Street
Delta, CO 84146

12 GA. "FLECHETTE SHOT SHELLS"

A flechette is a small dart shaped projectile, that is clustered in an explosive warhead, dropped in a missile from an airplane or fired from a hand held weapon. One unique application of this 1 1/2" flechette was to load these in a 12 GA. shotgun for taking out snipers hiding in thick brush or trees. Due to the penetration of these projectiles, tree limbs and brush would not disperse the darts. Even if some were dispersed, this would still have an all-covering pattern within a tree or brush. Generally 20 of these darts are placed in each 12 GA. shell. (Cannot be shipped to California, Florida, or New York City addresses.) Requires Hazardous Materials charge of $8.00. 3 UNITS PER PACKAGE $11.95 / 3 PACKAGES FOR $29.95.

PHOENIX SYSTEMS INC.
PO Box 3339
Evergreen, CO 80437

12 ga. Flechette Shotshell

Finally available to the public. Developed by the US military to increase both the effective range and lethality of the shotgun in combat. The flechette darts are made like a sharpened steel nail, are 1/16" thick, 1 and 1/2" long and have 4 stabilizing tail fins for better flight characteristics. There are 20 flechettes in each cartridge and are much more effective than standard shot loads in close combat and in areas of heavy brush, as the flechettes are very difficult to deflect. Cartridges are packaged 3 to a pack. Cannot be shipped to California, Florida, or New York City. 2 and 3/4" Cartridge $14.95.

[351] The SLA is outfitted with older T-55 tanks. These tanks have a 100mm cannon which cannot fire the shells in question. According to UNIFIL, there are indications that some of the T-55 tanks may have been fitted with 105mm cannon (they are then designated TI-67), but it appears that these SLA tanks are not supplied with antipersonnel shells. Human Rights Watch telephone interview with a UNIFIL spokesman in Lebanon, October 23, 1995.

fuze for the M494, a U.S. manufactured 105mm, tank-fired antipersonnel shell. The fuze, and probably also the M494 shell, were apparently supplied to the Israeli military by the U.S. government.[352]

Lebanese doctors who have treated flechette victims assert that the darts have a devastating effect. While stressing that shrapnel from the indiscriminate firing of ordinary shells—a much more frequent occurrence—has caused more deaths and injuries in southern Lebanon, they point out that flechettes have caused serious injuries to civilians. In interviews in August 1995, they made the following observations:

- "The nail's rotation and its sharp, pointed head maximize the damage."
- "The spinning is what makes the flechette dangerous. And the smaller the nail, the more dangerous it is when it enters the body."
- "The speed of the nails allows them to penetrate one part of the body and move on to another, doing damage along the way."
- "When the nail enters the body, it is like a drill [because the tail end is spinning]." (This doctor explained that the tail end does additional damage as the nail moves, ripping apart tissue as it spins).[353]

Two recent cases demonstrate the lethality of flechettes. On July 8, 1995, at about 9:15 p.m., four dart shells were fired at the five-room house of Khadija Bdeir, thirty-eight, in Nabatiyeh al-Fowqa. Three of her children died: Jihan, seventeen, Silvana, twelve, and Zakariya, four. Four more persons were injured: her daughter Rabab, sixteen, her son Abbas, ten, and neighbors Ali

---

[352] According to *Jane's Ammunition Handbook*, the U.S. Army was the only armed force to have procured this round. Jane's Information Group, *Jane's Ammunition Handbook 1993-94*, p. 134. The fuze, which was also manufactured in the U.S., makes it highly likely that this is indeed a U.S. manufactured and supplied shell. Reportedly the U.S. no longer manufactures the shell (though it continues to remain in U.S. inventory). Apparently Israel now produces its own 120mm version of this shell. Robert Fisk and UNIFIL sources claim that a fuze that was recovered from a 120mm shell in October 1994 had Israeli markings. See Robert Fisk, "Seven die in Israeli 'revenge' raid," *The Independent*, October 22, 1994, and UNIFIL, "Information concerning flechette shells used by IDF," January 23, 1995. An Israeli company, Reshef Technologies, does produce a fuze specifically designed for such a shell, the "Omega M127 Electronic Time Fuze." See Barbara Starr, "US test programme to assess ASRAAM," *Jane's Defense Weekly*, vol. 22, no. 17 (October 29, 1994), p. 18.

[353] Human Rights Watch interviews, southern Lebanon, August 1995.

Abbas, twelve, and Yahya Sabbagh, thirty-two. All of the victims had been
sitting outside the front door of their house when the shells exploded. Ms. Bdeir
said the attack was totally unexpected. "We have been living here for twelve
years and this house had never been shelled. They know us. They can see us,"
explained Ms. Bdeir, pointing to the Israeli military position on a nearby hilltop,
with an unobstructed view of her house. There had been no military activity in
the area and therefore no reason to expect danger, she claimed. If this had been
the case, she said, people would not have permitted their children to go outside.[354]

Jihan and Silvana were brought to Al-Janoub Hospital in Nabatiyeh.
Jihan died in the operating room. Dr. Ali Mansour, a cardiologist, said: "She
was in cardiac arrest, with a nail in her heart. She also had a nail in her back,
and holes in her legs. Ten doctors gathered and tried to give her first aid."
Silvana was also brought into the operating room. "She was in shock," Dr.
Mansour said. "Her abdomen was swollen. She had an abdominal haemorrhage.
We brought her directly to surgery and gave her three units of blood. She went
into a coma from the blood loss. The veins and arteries in her abdomen were cut
from the nails. After one hour, we transferred her to Ghassan Hammoud
Hospital in Sidon. She died several hours later."[355]

Zakariya, who was hit with seven flechettes in the head and nine in his
abdomen, died in the hospital several days later. Dr. Ali al-Hur, the
neurosurgeon who operated on Zakariya in al-Ra'i Hospital in Sidon, provided
medical details:

> The main damage was in his head. The CAT scan showed a
> nail in his brain, cerebral haemorrhage and cerebral edema.
> The nail entered on its side, not by its tip, and made damage
> across the brain, like scissors, because of its speed. We had
> planned to remove the nail and stop the bleeding but this was
> impossible because of the edema and a prolapse of the brain
> tissue. Finally, we could only stop the bleeding and close the
> brain. The nail stayed inside.

[354] Human Rights Watch interview, Nabatiyeh al-Fowqa, August 17, 1995.

[355] Human Rights Watch interview, Nabatiyeh, August 22, 1995.

Dr. al-Hur said that the four-year-old died of uremia.[356] The Israeli chief of staff, Lt.-Gen. Amnon Shahak, told Israeli Television the day following the attack: "Yesterday we fired at the wrong place in Nabatiyeh but that happens in the kind of war we are fighting there."[357]

A similar attack claimed the lives of four civilians and wounded another four when a number of flechette shells were fired at homes in Nabatiyeh al-Fowqa on October 19, 1994. First, four conventional shells damaged property in the village but caused no injuries; the dead and injured were hit by flechettes from shells that followed. The shelling began between 8:30 and 9:00 a.m. One eyewitness, Habib Atweh, who had been at the house of a relative at the time the shelling began, told Human Rights Watch: "I heard the shelling and went to the window. I saw the brightness of the cannon firing from Dabshe [an Israeli military position on a nearby hilltop, clearly visible from the village]." According to Mr. Atweh, four shells landed around his own house, which is located in a residential area, but no one was injured. The verandah wall and ceiling, and a concrete support column at the end of the verandah, were hit and damaged. One of the shells "came right through the house," he said. After the shells fell, residents gathered in the street, and Mr. Atweh and others entered his house to inspect the damage and see if anyone was injured. At this moment he and others were injured. "I was standing in the house and I felt a fire coming at me. It felt like I was hit on the right side, and I bumped into my son Hilal." Four relatives were killed immediately: his son Rabi'a, twenty-four; Husein Basal, a twelve-year-old nephew who was in a room off the verandah; Habib Ali Atweh, twenty-five, who lived in the house next door; and Qasem Basal, a twenty-six-year-old father of three. Mr. Atweh suffered a partially amputated index finger and injuries from one flechette that lodged in the right side of his face, one into his head behind his ear, and several in his stomach. The other three men injured were Mr. Atweh's son Hilal, twenty (flechettes in his abdomen and hip); Husein Ali Salman, twenty-eight (flechette removed from his spinal cord; two fingers of left hand amputated); and Ismail Basal, thirty (flechettes in neck).[358]

---

[356] Human Rights Watch interview, Sidon, August 23, 1995.

[357] "Israel says it killed Lebanese girls by mistake," Reuters, July 9, 1995.

[358] Human Rights Watch interview, Nabatiyeh, August 22, 1995. This attack was widely reported in the press. See, for example, "Lebanon: Israel uses banned shells in South Lebanon," Reuters, October 20, 1994.

There were additional civilian casualties, including one death, from flechettes in the village of Qabrikha in December 1995, following a guerrilla attack on a military target in the village of al-Qantara in the Israeli-occupied area. Hizballah retaliated by firing rockets into northern Israel. According to a U.N. report:

> On 29 December, the Islamic Resistance fired mortars to an IDF/DFF position at Al Qantarah. IDF retaliated with tank and artillery fire, using flechette antipersonnel munitions. One civilian was killed, four others were wounded and some houses in the village of Qabrikha were damaged. Several hours later, two salvos of rockets were fired into Israel, impacting around Qiryat Shemona and causing material damage.[359]

Not only civilians have been the targets of dart shells. In September 1994, the Irish UNIFIL battalion was hit by such a shell,[360] and on December 10, 1995 three Norwegian UNIFIL soldiers were wounded by flechette shells. In that particular attack, according to UNFIL, a total of six flechette tank rounds were fired toward the Norwegian patrol. At least two were Israeli-made 120mm shells, and at least two others were 105mm M494 U.S.-made rounds.[361]

Until recently, Israeli officials refused to acknowledge the IDF's use of these weapons. But earlier this year, after yet another Lebanese civilian was killed,[362] the Israeli minister of health, Ephraim Sneh, a former commander in southern Lebanon, admitted that flechette shells were in fact used by the IDF.[363]

---

[359] United Nations Security Council, *Report of the Secretary-General on the United Nations Interim Force in Lebanon*, S/1996/45 (January 22, 1996), par. 6(b).

[360] "Lebanon: death toll in South Lebanon shelling up to seven," Reuters, October 20, 1994.

[361] Human Rights Watch telephone interview with a UNIFIL spokesman in Lebanon, January 31, 1996.

[362] "Israeli anti-personnel shell kills civilian," Reuters, December 29, 1995. Hizballah reportedly fired more than ten Katyusha rockets at the northern Israeli town of Kiryat Shemona in retaliation; there were no reported injuries. "Hizbollah hits Israel in reprisal for shelling," Reuters, December 29, 1995.

[363] "Israel confirms it uses banned shells in Lebanon," Reuters, January 1, 1996.

VII. WEAPONS TRANSFERS AND THE CONFLICT IN SOUTHERN LEBANON

Arms to Israel

The United States is the major military patron for Israel, and Israel is by far the number one recipient of U.S. military aid. In all, Israel has received more than $40 billion in military aid from the U.S. No other country is remotely close to Israel's level of military aid.[364] The official objective of U.S. aid to Israel is laid out simply in the State Department's March 1996 foreign aid justification document: "The United States is committed to the maintenance of Israel's security and qualitative military advantage against any likely combination of adversaries....The commitment to Israel's security has been a cornerstone of U.S. Middle East policy since the creation of the State of Israel in 1948."[365]

At first, the U.S. was not a significant military supplier to Israel, although the U.S. discreetly encouraged allies such as France and Germany to provide major weapons systems. U.S. military assistance began to grow in the mid-1960s, and the relationship took on a new dimension in 1968 with the U.S. agreement to sell to Israel fifty F-4 Phantom fighter-bombers. This was at the time one of the most advanced fighter aircraft in the U.S. arsenal, and had up to that point been made available only to NATO allies.[366]

This qualitative (as well as quantitative) change in the U.S.-Israeli military relationship was in two important ways a product of the June War of 1967, in which Israel swiftly defeated Egypt, Syria and Jordan, and in the process occupied the Sinai Peninsula, the West Bank (including East Jerusalem) and the Gaza Strip, and the Golan Heights. First, the war and its outcome sharply increased the domestic political resonance of U.S.-Israeli relations. While the war in Vietnam was the dominant issue of the day, the sale of Phantom jets to

---

[364] Since World War II other top recipients are: Egypt $21 billion; South Vietnam $16 billion; Turkey $14 billion; South Korea $9 billion; and, Greece $8 billion. U.S. Agency for International Development, U.S. Overseas Loans and Grants, July 1, 1945-September 30, 1994 (1995), p. 13; Department of Defense Security Assistance Agency, Fiscal Year Series, As of September 30, 1993 (1994), pp. 106-107; U.S. Department of State, Congressional Presentation for Foreign Operations, Fiscal Year 1997 (March 1996), p. 424.

[365] Department of State, Congressional Presentation FY97, p. 417.

[366] Joe Stork, "Israel as a Strategic Asset," *MERIP Reports* (Washington, DC: Middle East Research and Information Project, May 1982), p. 4.

Israel became a leading issue in the Democratic presidential primaries (Senator Robert Kennedy's advocacy of the sale is held to have triggered his assassination at the hands of Sirhan Sirhan) and U.S. military sales to Israel remained an issue in the Nixon-Humphrey general election campaign.   Second, Israel's overwhelming military victory gave a significant boost to those in the U.S. national security establishment who regarded Israel as a potential "strategic asset" in the Cold War rivalry with the Soviet Union for influence in the Middle East, at a time that coincided with Britain's announcement that it intended to withdraw as a major military presence in the Persian Gulf .

The U.S.-Israeli military supply relationship has remained ever since a potentially significant "winning" issue in U.S. national politics. It acquired its strategic character beginning in the early 1970s, under the tutelage of Richard Nixon and Henry Kissinger. Between 1971 and 1973, U.S. military sales to Israel doubled over the previous three-year period, and this increased volume of sales became totally financed by U.S. government loans.[367]   In addition, the U.S. signed an initial memorandum of understanding for the transfer of U.S. technical information and assistance to allow Israel to develop a sophisticated military manufacturing capacity of its own.

The level of sales and aid skyrocketed as a result of the October War of 1973. New arms sales agreements with Israel totaled $2.3 billion in FY1974 alone, and these sales were financed for the first time with $1.5 billion in grant aid, as well as nearly $1 billion in loans.[368]   Since the signing of the Camp David Accords in 1978, high levels of military and economic aid to Israel and Egypt have been the central feature of the U.S. foreign aid program.

For each of the past ten years, Congress has appropriated $1.8 billion in military grants for Israel.[369]   In the most recent fiscal year, FY1996, Israel's $1.8 billion represented 56 percent of all U.S. military aid. Israel has long received preferential treatment from the Congress and from both Democratic and Republican Administrations. Examples of this include the fact that traditionally

---

[367] U.S. sales grew very rapidly from the mid-1960s through the mid-1970s, as shown by this progression: 1962-64=$4 million; 1965-67=$140 million; 1968-70=$530 million; 1971-73=$957 million; 1974-76=$4.3 billion. DSAA, Fiscal Year Series, (1994), pp. 106-107.

[368] DSAA, Fiscal Year Series, (1994), pp. 106.

[369] DSAA, Fiscal Year Series, (1994), pp. 106;   Department of State, Congressional Presentation, FY1997 (March 1996), p. 424.

Israel has been one of the few nations to receive military aid as a grant—most receive loans;[370] Israel alone, by law, receives its military aid within thirty days of the passage of the foreign aid bill;[371] Israel is one of the only nations for which Congress still "earmarks" (requires by law) a certain level of military aid (only Israel and Egypt were earmarked in FY1996); Israel is allowed to spend U.S. military aid not just to buy U.S. arms, but also for procurement of Israeli manufactured arms; and, until recently, Israel was one of just a handful of nations allowed to spend U.S. military aid on purchases directly from private U.S. manufacturers as well as from the U.S. government.[372]

In addition to the annual $1.8 billion appropriation, Congress created a special $700 million drawdown account for Israel in 1990 which it could use to buy U.S. weapons, especially those the Pentagon was retiring from Europe.[373] President Clinton added another $161.9 million to the account in March 1994 to enable Israel to purchase fifty F-16A/B fighter planes. Earlier major purchases from this fund included twenty-four Apache and ten Blackhawk helicopters, and ten F-15A/B fighters.[374]

During the course of the 1990s, U.S. military assistance has been used primarily for the procurement of and follow-on support for F-15 and F-16 fighter aircraft, F-4 fighter aircraft upgrades, Apache attack helicopters, SAAR corvettes, and the Israeli-produced Merkava tank. Funds have also been used to enhance Israeli intelligence gathering and early warning capabilities.[375] The State

---

[370] U.S. military aid to Israel has been all grant since Fiscal Year 1985.

[371] This early disbursement allows Israel to invest and earn interest on some of the money prior to spending it on arms or debt service. This can amount to tens of millions of dollars each year.

[372] The Pentagon terminated use of military aid for commercial purchases in January 1994 due to "program weaknesses." General Accounting Office, GAO/NSIAD-93-184, "Military Sales to Israel and Egypt: DoD Needs Stronger Controls over U.S.-Financed Procurements," July 1993, p. 3.

[373] Public Law 101-513, 104 Stat. 2064, Sec. 599B, November 5, 1990.

[374] Federation of American Scientists, *Arms Sales Monitor*, no. 25, April 30, 1994, p. 9.

[375] See the State Department's Congressional Presentation Documents for Fiscal Years 90-97.

Department has indicated that the aid funds requested for FY1997 will be used for "major multi-year procurement programs, such as new F-15I fighter aircraft purchases, SAAR corvettes, and continued upgrades of Israel's Apache and Blackhawk helicopter squadrons."[376]

Owing to this generosity of the U.S., Israel also ranks as one of the biggest customers for U.S. arms sales. Over the past five years, Israel has purchased nearly $4 billion in U.S. weapons, equipment and defense services.[377] The U.S. Government estimates that over the next two years (FY1996-97), Israel will buy $890 million in arms through the government-to-government sales channel, and $1.4 billion through the private commercial sales channel.[378] While most top buyers such as Saudi Arabia pay for the arms with their own funds, Israeli arms buys from the U.S. are in essence paid for by the U.S. taxpayer.[379] Israel's Ministry of Defense has a purchasing mission in New York, staffed by more than 200 personnel, that processes about 20,000 purchase orders from the U.S. annually.[380]

---

[376] State Department, Congressional Presentation FY97, p. 425.

[377] Only Saudi Arabia, Taiwan, Turkey, Japan, South Korea, Egypt, and Kuwait have purchased more U.S. arms from FY1991-95. U.S. military sales to Israel total $24 billion since FY1954, including $18 billion in government-to-government sales and $6 billion in private commercial sales. DSAA, Fiscal Year Series, p. 106; State Department Congressional Presentation Documents FY1996 and 1997.

[378] State Department, Congressional Presentation FY97, pp. 457, 464.

[379] A significant portion of U.S. military grants each year are used by Israel not to buy weapons but to service its debt to the U.S. from military loans made prior to 1985. In the 1990s, there have been several investigations into fraud and abuse of U.S. security assistance to Israel. In 1991, for example, Israel convicted Air Force General Rami Dotan of skimming an estimated $40 million in U.S. funds by submitting false purchase orders on U.S.-financed contracts. A senior official of the General Electric Company was also involved and GE agreed to a settlement with the Department of Justice involving payment of $69 million in civil damages and criminal penalties. Since the Dotan affair DoD auditors have uncovered evidence that in a number of contracts awarded by Israel, contractors may have improperly used U.S. military aid funds to pay questionable commissions and to reimburse foreign officials for travel expenses. General Accounting Office, GAO/NSIAD-93-184, "Military Sales to Israel and Egypt: DoD Needs Stronger Controls over U.S.-Financed Procurements," July 1993, pp. 2- 4.

[380] General Accounting Office, "Military Sales to Israel..." July 1993, pp. 9-10.

Israel has purchased a full range of weaponry from the United States, including fighter, transport, tanker, reconnaissance and early warning aircraft; attack and transport helicopters; tanks; armored personnel carriers; self-propelled and towed artillery; multiple rocket launchers; air defense guns; surface-to-air, surface-to-surface, air-to-surface, air-to-air, antiship and antitank missiles; mortars; machine guns, assault rifles, and ammunition. As noted in the previous chapter, the U.S. may have provided phosphorus shells, and flechette shells which have been misused in southern Lebanon.

The weaponry that Israel has used most extensively in violations of the laws of war in southern Lebanon are fighter aircraft, attack helicopters, and artillery. As the supplier of much of this weaponry, the U.S. must share the responsibility for its misuse. Israel has about 400 U.S.-supplied fighter aircraft in its inventory, including 205 F-16 and seventy-five F-4 ground attack planes.[381] Press accounts indicate that the F-16 and F-4 were both used extensively during Operation Accountability. According to the International Institute for Strategic Studies, Israel's attack helicopters are exclusively U.S.-supplied: forty-two AH-64A Apache, thirty-nine AH-1F Cobra, and thirty-five Hughes 500MD.[382] Human Rights Watch has documented attacks by Israeli helicopters on civilians and ambulances during Operation Accountability. The bulk of Israeli artillery is U.S.-supplied, although Israel produces its own and has other non-U.S. guns as well. Israel appears to have about 1,000 U.S.-made artillery pieces, including 155mm M109 self-propelled, 175mm M107 self-propelled, 203mm M110 self-propelled, 105mm M101/2 towed, and 155mm M114 towed howitzers.[383] Israel has stated that two types of artillery pieces were used during Operation Accountability: M109 howitzers and M110 howitzers.[384] Most civilian casualties in southern Lebanon over the years have been caused by IDF/SLA shelling, especially during Operation Accountability.

---

[381] International Institute for Strategic Studies, *The Military Balance 1995-96* (London: Oxford University Press, 1995), p. 137.

[382] IISS, p. 137.

[383] Ibid., p. 136, and *Jane's Armour and Artillery 1993-94* (Surrey: Jane's Information Group Limited, 1994), p. 674.

[384] Col. Ahaz Ben-Ari, head of the IDF's international law branch, in a communication to Human Rights Watch, May 18, 1994.

U.S. arms sales and deliveries to Israel—and other nations in the region—escalated in the aftermath of the Gulf War. According to one arms control organization, the U.S. agreed to deliver the following to Israel between August 1990 and July 1993: 525 Hellfire antitank missiles, fifteen F-15A/B aircraft, 300 AIM-9S Sidewinder missiles, ten Patriot air defense launchers and 129 Patriot missiles.[385] Other notable recent sales include twenty F-15I fighter aircraft, fifty F-16 fighter aircraft (mentioned above), ten S-70/UH-60 Blackhawk helicopters, six M-577A2 armored personnel carriers, six 227mm Multiple Launch Rocket Systems (MRLS), 300 AIM-9S Sidewinder air-to-air missiles, and an unknown number of FIM-92A Stinger surface-to-air missiles.[386] In the spring of 1995, the Administration notified Congress of the sale of an unspecified number of Hellfire II antitank missiles, valued at $45 million, and forty-two MRLS launchers with 305 rocket pods.[387]

Israel has also received weapons under the Excess Defense Articles (EDA) program, a program under which defense articles no longer needed by the U.S. military are transferred free of charge or at a reduced rate. In FY96, Congress was notified of proposed deliveries of fourteen AH-1E Cobra helicopters and 30,000 M16A1 rifles. In FY95, Congress was notified of proposed deliveries of nearly 35,000 M16A1 rifles, 1,500 M2 machine guns, and 2,469 M204 grenade launchers.[388] In FY94, Congress was notified of proposed deliveries of, among other things, 30,000 rounds of M456A2 105mm HEP-T tank ammunition, and howitzer parts.[389]

The U.S.-Israeli military relationship goes beyond dollars and arms. The closeness of the relationship is indicated by the State Department's recent statement that one of the objectives of its aid program is to help in "reformulating

---

[385] Arms Control Association, *U.S. Arms Transfers to the Middle East Since the Invasion of Kuwait*, August 11, 1993, p. 1.

[386] Stockholm International Peace Research Institute, *SIPRI Yearbook 1995* (Oxford: Oxford University Press, 1995), p. 527.

[387] Federation of American Scientists, *Arms Sales Monitor*, no. 30, July 20, 1995, p. 10.

[388] Department of Defense Excess Defense Articles computer bulletin board.

[389] Federation of American Scientists, *Arms Sales Monitor*, no. 25, March 15, 1994, p. 9, and no. 24, April 30, 1994, p. 9.

Israeli defense thinking, strategy and doctrine."[390] Israel is also one of the few nations outside of NATO where the U.S. stockpiles arms for potential use in regional conflicts (South Korea and Thailand are others).[391] Israel has benefited greatly from the sharing of intelligence and technology by the U.S. The most notable current long-term joint military initiatives are the "Arrow" anti-tactical ballistic missile program and the acquisition of advanced, long-range U.S. F-15I fighter aircraft.[392] The U.S. has also played an important role in building Israel's domestic defense industry into one of the most sophisticated not just in the developing world, but anywhere. Reflecting its military production prowess, Israel has long been recognized as one of the biggest exporters of arms in the developing world.

While Israel continues to rely primarily on the United States, it has increasingly entered into cooperative defense arrangements with other nations in recent years, including China and many former Warsaw Pact nations, such as Russia, Ukraine, Poland, Romania and the Czech Republic, as well as France, Germany, Turkey, India, Singapore, Thailand and South Africa.[393] While the success of the peace process in the Middle East has made it politically possible for Israel to expand its military ties, the strength of its defense industry, and its ability to upgrade former Soviet equipment, have made it appealing to other nations.

Major Israeli arms acquisitions in recent years from countries other than the United States include:[394]

---

[390] State Department, Congressional Presentation FY97, p. 425.

[391] The FY1996 foreign aid appropriations bill permits additions to stockpiles in Israel without additional legislation (previously allowable only for stockpiles for NATO purposes). State Dept., Congressional Presentation FY97, p. 476.

[392] State Department, Congressional Presentation FY97, p. 425.

[393] See, for example, "Peace Widens Israel's Markets," *Jane's Defence Weekly*, November 19, 1994, p. 23, and "Peace Process Nets Israel New Recognition," *Defense News*, July 25-31, 1994, p. 4.

[394] See tables in the last five editions of the annual Stockholm International Peace Research Institute, *SIPRI Yearbook* (Oxford: Oxford University Press).

- Germany: two Dolphin-class submarines, fifty BRDM-2 scout cars, eight Tpz-1 armored personnel carriers, twelve T-72 tanks, and SA-6 surface-to-air missile systems
- Russia: forty-five BRDM-2 scout cars
- France: four AS-565A Panther anti-submarine helicopters
- The Netherlands: Patriot surface-to-air missile system.

Arms to Hizballah

It is frequently alleged that Hizballah has received most of its weaponry from Iran, through Syria, although few details are publicly available. The main accusations have been made by government officials in Israel and the U.S., which has been Israel's main supporter in the conflict with Hizballah. At a U.S. congressional hearing held during the week of Operation Accountability in 1993, then U.S. Assistant Secretary of State for Near Eastern and South Asian Affairs Edward Djerejian noted that Iran is "Hezbollah's main patron."[395] When asked by Rep. Lee Hamilton about Syria's role and its ability "to stop Hizballah," Mr. Djerejian replied, "...in terms of Hezbollah's presence in the very south of Lebanon, there they act rather autonomously because there are no Lebanese armed forces or Syrian troops there....But where the question arises is Hezbollah's ability to rearm, to obtain logistical support, to obtain the funding and all the support it gets from Iran. There is a question which involves other parties and also Syria's influence on what it can do about that."[396] He also said, "We have had very in depth discussions with the Syrian leadership and with the Lebanese leadership, to have them do whatever they can to control, to try to influence, and to at least stop the resupply of Hezbollah in Lebanon."[397]

Hizballah's arsenal has been reported to include armored personnel carriers, multiple rocket launchers, rocket launchers, recoilless launchers, antitank weapons (including the AT-3 Sagger guided missile), antiaircraft guns,

---

[395] "Developments in the Middle East July 1993," Hearing before the House Committee on Foreign Affairs, July 27, 1993 (Washington: U.S. Government Printing Office, 1993), p. 13.

[396] Ibid.

[397] Ibid., p. 19. See also, Michael Eisenstadt, "Syria and the Terrorist Connection," *Jane's Intelligence Review*, vol. 5, no. 1 (January 1993), p. 33, which states that Syria has been complicit in Iran's arming of Hizballah by permitting Hizballah to receive arms from Iran through the Damascus International Airport.

SA-7 antiaircraft missiles, and a wide range of light weapons and small arms such as rocket-propelled grenades, machine guns, assault rifles, grenades, and landmines.[398] *Jane's Intelligence Review* has reported that Iran supplied Milan antitank missiles to Hizballah, and possibly also U.S. Stinger shoulder-fired antiaircraft missiles obtained from Afghanistan.[399] *Jane's* also reports that "over one-third of [Iran's] financial support for liberation movements abroad is allocated to Lebanese Hezbollah via its embassies in Beirut and Damascus."[400]

Also according to *Jane's*, Iran supplied Hizballah with BM-21 rocket launchers—commonly known as Katyushas—throughout the 1980s.[401] The 122mm BM-21 Grad multiple rocket launcher, otherwise known as a Katyusha, was first produced in the former Soviet Union in the 1950s. It has since been produced in many nations with many variations. Perhaps the most common version of the Katyusha is a forty round rocket system carried on a truck. There is also a twelve round system (the Grad-V) and a thirty-six round system (Grad-I). All of these basic BM-21s can be fired either singly or in a salvo.[402]

According to Israel, the majority of Katyushas fired into Israel during Operation Accountability were from single round launchers "manufactured in China and North Korea as well as in Iran."[403] The BM-21-P is a single round

___

[398] Edward C. Ezell, *Small Arms World Report*, vol. 4, no. 4 (December 1993), p. 26, and International Institute for Strategic Studies, *The Military Balance 1995-96* (London: Oxford University Press, 1995), p. 140.

[399] Magnus Ranstorp, "Hezbollah's Future?" *Jane's Intelligence Review*, vol. 7, no. 1 (January 1995), p. 35. Ranstorp also reported that Syria had tried to limit shipments of arms from Iran to Hizballah in a meeting of Iran's minister of intelligence and Syria's chief of staff in Beirut in late 1994, and added: "Hezbollah circumvents these limits through the purchase of advanced weaponry, particularly AT-3s, from various arms dealers in Lebanon. Even if arms shipments from Iran ceased, it is estimated that Hezbollah has an arsenal that would enable it to continue its current level of military activity for at least five years." Ibid.

[400] Ibid., p. 34.

[401] Ibid.

[402] *Jane's Armour and Artillery 1993-94*, p. 598.

[403] Col. Ahaz Ben-Ari, head of the IDF's international law branch, in a communication to Human Rights Watch, May 18, 1994.

launcher system which consists of a tube and a tripod, weighing a total of 50 kilograms. The launch tube is 2.4 meters long. It fires two rounds per minute and can be reloaded manually in thirty seconds. It takes three minutes to set up the system and thirty seconds to break it down. It has a maximum range of about 11,000 meters.[404] Iran produces a variation of the Katyusha—the 122mm NOOR multiple artillery rocket system—that is believed to be available as a single round lightweight launcher.[405]

[404] *Jane's Armour and Artillery 1993-94*, p. 598.

[405] Ibid., p. 613.